Ties-Ties-Ties

Traditional Quilts from Neckties

by

Janet B. Elwin

American Quilter's Society

P. O. Box 3290 • Paducah, KY 42002-3290

Located in Paducah, Kentucky, the American Quilter's Society (AQS), is dedicated to promoting the accomplishments of today's quilters. Through its publications and events, AQS strives to honor today's quiltmakers and their work – and inspire future creativity and innovation in quiltmaking.

Library of Congress Cataloging-in-Publication Data

Elwin, Janet B.
      Ties–ties–ties : traditional quilts from neckties / by Janet B. Elwin.
         p. cm.
      Includes bibliographical references.
      ISBN 0-89145-864-6
      1. Quilting–Patterns.   2. Neckties.   I. Title.
TT835.E475 1996
746.46'041–dc20   96-12347
                                                      CIP

Additional copies of this book may be ordered from: American Quilter's Society, P.O. Box 3290, Paducah, KY 42002-3290 @ $19.95. Add $2.00 for postage & handling.

Copyright: 1996, Janet B. Elwin

Printed in USA.

Dedication

"At times our own light goes out and is rekindled by a spark from another person. Each of us has cause to think with deep gratitude of those who have lighted the flame within us."

Albert Schweitzer

With that in mind, I would like to dedicate this book to three people who have kept my flame alive and encouraged the thrift shop forays:

Mabelle Estelle Burr Beres, my mother, 1910 – 1986;

Eva Hope Hoyt Maze, Bud's grandmother, 1896 – 1988; and

Florence Anna Maze Elwin, Bud's mother, 1915 –

Acknowledgments

Since my mother, Gram, Florence, and I have spent many happy hours gleaning treasures from thrift shops, they instilled in me a love to recycle whatever I could (Gram once bought a car at a yard sale). As I look over my quilts featured in this book, not only were the ties recycled, but so were most of the background fabrics as well. Never dreaming all these "found" objects would work so well together, I am now a little sad that I have used almost everything up. But not to worry – tomorrow there will be another guild giving away drapery samples, another friend giving me ties, and another day for Florence and me to prowl through the thrift shops looking for something just right. My deepest gratitude to all who have participated in this project:

Friend Phyllis for tons of shirting fabrics;

Orange Grove Quilters Guild, Garden Grove, California, for boxes of drapery samples;

M/M Urayama, Takaraya Co., Ltd., Sendai City, Japan for new tie fabrics;

Betty Ann Watts of Communications Concepts, representing Madeira threads and Mundial scissors;

Freudenberg Nonwoven for Pellon® products;

Hobbs Bonded Fibers for batting;

Pfaff for their Creative 7550 sewing machine;

Omnigrid, Inc. for rulers;

The guest quilters who are sharing their grand works and techniques with all of us in this book.

To all who have contributed ties:

Cynthia and Bill; Judy and Tom; Donna and Frank; George; Ed; Dana; Sal; Al; Rhoda and Lee; the members of the U-U Fellowship, Edgecomb, Maine; Beverly; Jan; Lois and all her kids at school; Sue; students in my classes; Charlotte and Gene; Whitney; Celia, Pam, and John, Anne, Pat, and Rosamund of the United Kingdom; Ann-Marie of France; Mary; the Thursday Quilters; George and Pearl; Ed and Sally; George and Norma; Jane and Dick; the student from Kansas who sent me the box of vintage ties; Robin and Tom; Marie and Louise, also of the United Kingdom; Polly and Ed; Dave and Bill whose contributions were unending, and mostly to Bud, my husband, partner, business associate, social director, and now chief cook and bottle washer, my everlasting thanks and love. If any contributors' names were omitted, please forgive me, but know that your ties were received with grateful acceptance and put to good use.

Contents

Chapter

1

This Ain't A New Idea

VICTORIAN CRAZY QUILT

60" x 60", maker unknown, c.1900,
gift of Florence Elwin, in the Elwin collection.

NECKTIES, you ask? Why on earth would any-one even think of using neckties in quilts? Why not? Our quilting ancestors were extremely thrifty people and fabrics were always a challenge to them. We have seen many quilts made of used clothing. Our forefathers recycled everything. Many old clothes went right back into garments for members of the family, leaving behind scraps for quilts.

Some quilts made from recycled clothing were strictly utilitarian and very sturdy, but every now and then we come across a real beauty. The quilts we think of as first using silks and satins, including neckties, are the Victorian crazy quilts. These were quilts made mostly for fun, but each quiltmaker took great pains to create beautiful blocks with lots of creative stitches. Most of these quilts used bits and pieces of very lovely neckties.

Another quilt pattern that we see with a lot of suiting, tie, and shirting fabrics is the Log Cabin. Some of these antique Log Cabin quilts are rather somber in color with lots of grays, browns, and blacks. Many working people of days gone by had

ANTIQUE LOG CABIN

66" x 61", maker unknown, c. 1910,
gift of Florence Elwin, in the Elwin collection.

only their one "best" suit and the color was basic black. This made most of these quilts very conservative, but every once in a while a creative quiltmaker added pieces of satin, grosgrain, and silk, most likely scraps from ladies' gowns. These scraps brightened up these Log Cabin quilts considerably, as in the one shown.

My absolute favorite is the Log Cabin Hexagon variation shown on page 12. This quilt was a gift from a neighbor who knows I love quilts and who wanted to give it a good home. It originated in

Damariscotta, Maine, and is particularly appealing to me because the hexagon shape and the color yellow are both high on my list of favorites, so what a coincidence that this quilt, made so long ago, should fall into my hands.

But, it wasn't any one of these quilts that tempted me to use neckties on a broad scale. It was, in fact, a skirt. I have been designing and making patchwork skirts since 1980, and one of the first three designs I marketed in 1985 was a gored type with hexagon patchwork at the bottom. I made this

ANTIQUE LOG CABIN HEXAGON
53" x 81", maker unknown, c.1920,
gift of Ann Day, in the Elwin collection.

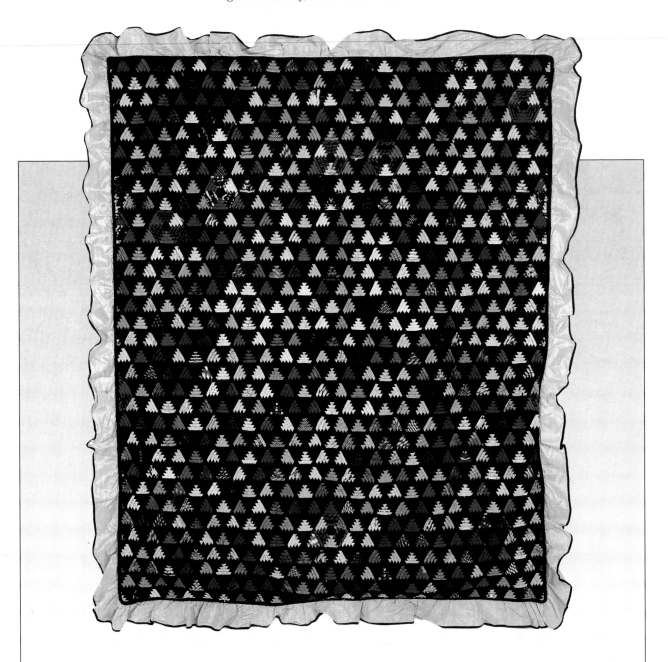

skirt (1985) for my own use plus a few to sell at a wholesale quilt market. It was a huge success because of its sophisticated style which could be made with very dressy fabrics or with cottons. One of my customers asked if it could be made with neckties. Well, I certainly didn't see why not. I began collecting wine-colored neckties to try this project. The skirt was beautiful and an immediate conversation starter wherever I wore it.

The next year at the Houston Quilt Market I redesigned the skirt pattern (1986) and again several years later (1989). The skirt is especially fun to wear at cocktail parties where men question me about the ties. After making and selling many skirts, I accumulated a lot of scraps but not many whole ties remained. This subsequently led to my large collection of tie fabrics. I first stored them in a shoebox, thinking of making a vest. Then that grew to a basket, and now it is a serious collection stored by color and texture.

With all these ties, I decided to move from skirts to quilts. I had made quite a few Dresden Plate wallhangings (see one in Chapter 5) so this seemed to me a very natural design to work with as it would highlight the ties as "ties." A 1930's Dresden Plate quilt was on my bed when I was a child and I always called the pieces of the plate "ties."

So I began with a Dresden Plate variation (HAPPY FATHER'S DAY shown on page 14), all pieced. While watching the Gulf War TV coverage, I cut 320 neckties for this masterpiece project. Unfortunately this still didn't make much of a dent in my tie collection. I resolved to use the rest on the reverse side of the quilt. I still had ties left over.

I succumbed to the entire syndrome when two friends came back from a yard sale with yet another bag of ties. What could I do? I just gave in and decided to see what I could do with all these ties.

This really is a recycled idea with recycled fabric. Wouldn't our quilting ancestors love it?

Since I started on my necktie adventures, I have discovered other reasons to make quilts with ties, rather than with the usual cotton quilting fabrics. Because of the richness of the fabrics, neckties make an ordinary quilt very special. Most necktie fabrics are not available for purchase, so through our collecting of used ties we have a resource of some very unusual fabrics and patterns. Even some of the ugliest ties can be rich and glowing in a quilt. Also, it's a lot of fun working with all those

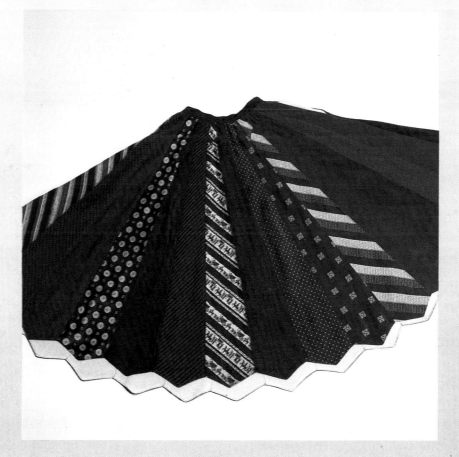

Janet Elwin's necktie skirt.

HAPPY FATHER'S DAY

60" x 68", by Janet B. Elwin, 1992,
machine pieced and quilted, in the Elwin collection.

stripes and geometrics that you see in ties. Making a quilt from ties is out of the ordinary – an exciting new challenge.

How Do You Get Them? – Sources for Ties

Searching for ties can be the most fun and also the most frustrating part of making quilts from neckties. There are countless people who already have bags, drawers, and closets full of ties and have no idea what to do with them. On the other hand, if you are like me, you might not have a single tie to start with. Here are some suggestions from my experience for getting a collection together.

Thrift Shops

My collection started with thrift shops. Thrift shops vary in price from shop to shop, but I have found recently that most of them are charging about $2 for a tie.

Rummage Sales & Yard Sales

These sales are another great source of cheap ties. One can often pick up a bag for next to nothing.

Church, Synagogue, and Fellowship Groups

I show my quilts at our fellowship congregation on holidays, special occasions, and sometimes just because I have finished a project I want to share. One Sunday during our announcement time, I made a request for neckties and got several donations the very next week.

Parties

Don't hesitate to let everyone know you are collecting neckties to use in quilts.

Friends and Family

Anytime you send a card, make a telephone call, or see a member of your family or your friends, *ask*.

Local Shops

I bought some really nice silk ties for my husband Bud (not for me). They were inexpensive, but I still couldn't justify them for my quilts quite yet. While going through the ties in the store, I noticed quite a few that were damaged and knew the store would never be able to sell them. I talked with the saleslady and made her an offer to buy them at $1 each. When I used those ties, I just marked the defects and cut around them. Sometimes you have to be bold and speak right up.

Husbands, Boyfriends, Significant Others

Raid their closets.

Dads, Grandads, Uncles

If these members of your family are in the retirement age group, they are a great source.

Tie Yardage

There are a few stores where you can buy tie fabric.

I'm sure I have left out a source you may know of, so get out there and look for ties. Beg from everyone. Lots of folks have heaps of ties they don't want to toss out and now they have you to give them to. Once you get into collecting ties, you might specialize in certain styles or eras or special fabrics.

While you are out on your quilt tie search, don't forget the other treasures in those thrift shops. Look for shirts (see STARRY STARRY TIES, Chapter 6), buttons, and drapery samples. You can also check your local decorating shop to see if they are tossing out those sample books. Look through the dress and skirt sections in thrift shops for fabulous cotton prints, and in the men's casual shirts for plaids. There is lots of gleaning to do in the recycling area.

Sprinkled throughout this book are the works of eleven guest quilters who made quilts with ties. They were asked to fill out questionnaires regarding how, when, and why they got involved in quilt/tie projects. Rhoda Cohen had a wonderful comment that I thought would be helpful for you. In her words, "The use of tie fabric on the diagonal gives excitement, drama, movement – causing a pleasurable tension. Neckties are designed to lend vitality to the otherwise static symmetry of a man's costume. Using reclaimed necktie fabric brings into play vestiges of the necktie's former life. Ties are personal choices of the men who wear them. A tie says *volumes* about the wearer."

Remember those thoughts as you search through your treasure trove of neckties, looking for just the right tie for your projects. Once upon a time some person bought this tie – perhaps its owner or perhaps the wife, girlfriend, or child – to adorn the body and complement the costume of a loved one. Many of the ties in your collection may not be to your taste, but I have found mixing beautiful, ugly and mundane make the quilt sparkle.

Depending on your skills and patience, beautiful results can be achieved using the techniques described in this book.

You might worry that working with tie fabrics may be difficult. Some people have absolutely no patience for fabrics that are not on-grain. Since I use anything (I look for color, pattern, and then the type of fabric), I have tried a lot of different techniques over the years. All those techniques have come into play for me since I have concentrated on ties. There are several techniques discussed in this book which will help you tame any unruly tie fabric.

The guest quilters have come up with some of their own techniques while working with ties. Each quilt project can be done using any number of the techniques covered in Chapter 2. Every project is laid out with the techniques used by the quiltmaker. In some cases, an easier way to do something was discovered and this was a recommendation – even though the quiltmaker hadn't actually done it. I have not tried to change or elaborate on any of the guest quilters' projects. The instructions are in their words. If you like one of their projects, but would rather use a technique from instructions for another quilt, please feel free to make changes and/or your own improvements. This has been a learning experience for all of us.

The projects in this book range from small wallhangings to large bed quilts – something for everybody. Some of the projects list specific necktie colors, patterns, and fiber contents to work with. Use these as suggestions and make your own choices from your collection. You can make any of the creative projects in this book, or you can adapt the ideas and techniques to purchased patterns or your own designs to make quilts, crafts, stuffed animals, or clothing.

The more you work with ties, the more ideas you will get. It's fun to search for that elusive tie or to find just the right project to showcase your collection of fabulous ties from family members, friends, or just your own gleanings.

Chapter

2

How Do You Prepare and Use Them?

My students and quilters in general have asked me, "What do you do with ties? How do you use them?" When I first started hearing those questions, I had only used some fabulous silk ties in a few different skirt patterns. In my Mariner's Compass skirt pattern, the ties looked beautiful and I had no trouble working with them, so these questions seemed perplexing as I didn't see why quilters couldn't use tie fabric in any pattern available.

Of course, until this point I had only used a tie here and there and never made a quilt in which over 50% of the fabric was ties of all different materials and weights. Herein lies the challenge of how to handle tie fabric – not which pattern to use because I can visualize any pattern in ties. Most quilters learn "rules" in the classroom and as I was self-taught, I had never heard quilters were supposed to use only 100% cotton. Therefore, I used whatever fabric I came across that looked attractive for the project I was working on. I believe that's why I am more tolerant of non-cotton fabrics. Besides, there is just too much great stuff out there in addition to 100% cotton.

Preparing the Ties

Before we dive into quilt patterns, we have to prepare our ties. Tie fabric, unlike cotton, needs a little special treatment before it is ready for the quilt.

Taking the Ties Apart

I start at the narrow end. Use a seam ripper or razor blade and open the seam about 3". If you are lucky, you will be able to pull the seam thread and it will unravel in a flash. The majority of ties come apart quickly and easily, but on occasion you come across a stubborn one – you will have to cut apart the entire length with your seam ripper or razor blade. Remove the linings from the ends of the ties. Toss these out along with the interfacing unless you can reuse them in making new ties or know of some other redeeming purpose for them.

Laundering

If you have ties that are precious and you are unsure of the end result, perhaps hand washing or dry cleaning would be the best, however, I wash everything.

Toss the opened ties into the washing machine. I throw everything in together, only separating the light from the dark ties. I use a gentle cycle which works fine if you are washing silk and wool ties along with polyester ones. Put the ties in a laundry bag or pillow case. If using a pillow case, close it with an elastic band. Some of the ties will ravel, so putting them in a bag will prevent a giant mess when you open the washing machine.

CAUTION: I don't dry clean ties because the cleaners do not always get the spots out, plus dry cleaning is expensive. But, and this is a big but, if you make a wallhanging, quilt, or any of the other projects in this book, my recommendation is to dry clean the finished piece. Even though you prewash your ties, that doesn't mean they will be colorsafe. Many of the dark ties will still run after washing. The main purpose of washing the ties to begin with is to remove the soil and stains.

Ties that run can work in your favor and be quite attractive, but if you are unhappy, toss them back into the washing machine with some powdered fabric bleach. I let them soak a bit, then wash. The ties that seem to cause the most problems are yellow ties with blue designs. I soak them in fabric bleach which seems to solve the problem.

Drying

Put all the ties in the dryer except the wool ones. The ties will twist up and ravel again in the dryer, but pull them apart and you will have some beautifully clean ties.

Ironing

This step is very important because this is the time to look over each and every tie. Carefully look for spots or defects.

You can spray a little spray starch or sizing onto the soft ties to give them a little body. This may be all the body they need for sewing. You may find creases sometimes will not come out. This can be caused by age and/or fading. Misting with water and then ironing again will save some ties. If that doesn't help, save them anyway. Look at the reverse side of the fabric. In some cases the creases are not noticeable and the fabric is perfectly fine. You can use the reverse sides for binding also.

Stains and Other Problems

If you find a tie that is still stained after the washing, put a spot remover on the spot, let it set a minute or two (follow the directions found on the back of the spot remover container), and then wash it again. In the washing machine, magic may be performed, but if the spot still won't budge, work around it. Just don't give up.

Another problem that may occur is some manufacturers adhere the labels with glue that doesn't come off. Cut around those areas or use the reverse side of the fabric if you can.

Once in awhile you have to get rid of a tie or two. It might have fallen apart from age. It's sad but true that some of these silk ties and other fancy fabrics deteriorate with time. So get rid of anything that is shredding. You can work around stains, but not disintegrating fabrics.

Sorting the Ties

Depending on how many ties you have, this sorting can be as simple as tossing them into a basket or as complicated as using boxes for separate colors. I started with the basket, then moved to individual plastic containers, sorting by color. Now I have graduated to two separate lots. I separate my ties by fabric, putting all the silks and lightweight fancy fabrics by color into individual containers. All the polyesters are sorted by color into individual other containers.

Using Interfacing

Many neckties are polyester or other medium weight fabrics which have plenty of body and are fairly easy to work with. However, lightweight (in other words, sleazy) ties, especially silk, work much better when you apply interfacing to the reverse side. I recommend Pellon® Easy-Shaper® which is a fusible interfacing for light to medium weight fabrics. If you fuse them to interfacing, you can cut the neckties any way you like, treating them as if they were cut on-grain. The interfacing stabilizes the tie fabric and prevents stretching on the bias.

To stabilize heavier weight tie fabric, use Pellon® fusible interfacing for medium weight to heavy weight fabrics. This will make a heavier tie, but again you can treat it as regular fabric. Most heavier weight ties used in my quilts have not been stabilized except when working with curves. However, if you are new to working with ties and are afraid of bias edges, stabilize.

I adhere interfacing to about half of the tie (do more than you need) and then cut the pieces I need.

All of the above sounds pretty simple, and it is, but it does take time. I almost always take my ties apart while watching TV. Don't forget to take a bag to your quilt guild (or any other kind of) meeting. In fact, the more people who see you working with ties, the more chances you have of acquiring more ties.

Using Ties in Quilts

The following are some general instructions for working with ties. You will find more details in the instructions for the quilts featured in this book.

In this section you will learn several methods of cutting and sewing tie fabric. There are two primary differences in using ties, compared to traditional quilting cotton. First, the stripes and diagonal patterns common in tie fabrics offer a special opportunity to play with the design when creating a quilt block. Second, handling tie fabrics both in cutting and piecing can be a challenge.

Grainline is important for both the design and the construction of blocks. My goal is to help you ease the sewing, keeping both the "tie look" and your sanity.

Another challenge is working with pieces of fabric the size of a necktie, rather than ordinary yardage. You may have to be creative when cutting from these narrow pieces of tie fabric, especially when cutting long strips for lattices or borders. It is OK to piece scraps together when needed.

Tester Block

Always make a tester block before you cut out an entire quilt of the same block. Some fabrics work just fine when stitching bias to straight of the grain and others will not cooperate as well. That is why it is so important to cut one block and stitch it together to see how it works. If the fabrics bunch or pucker, try cutting background fabrics as well as the tie fabrics off-grain. There are other solutions such as using foundation piecing. It would be wise to read all of these options in this chapter and also look to see how the guest quilters solved their problems. You can do it!

Cutting the Ties

You can cut templates with or without seam allowance or cut squares and triangles with a rotary cutter. I always make my tester block using templates without seam allowance. I like the accuracy of stitching on a marked sewing line. After I piece my block together in this manner and see how the pieces fit together, then I decide whether I will continue in this method (a must for intricate patterns such as Mariner's Compass) or switch over to using templates including seam allowance.

Even if you usually piece using templates with seam allowance, you may want to try them without seam allowance, especially if you find you have trouble piecing slippery stretchy tie pieces.

Use template material of your choice. If you use plastic templates to cut triangles, you can clearly see which way your stripes are going before you trace and cut.

Templates with No Seam Allowance

This method is an excellent choice for beginners and for making a tester block.

- Make your templates the size of the finished piece without adding any seam allowance.
- Use a sandpaper board. This helps tame your slippery tie fabric. Buy a sandpaper board or make one by gluing a piece of 8½" x 11" fine sandpaper to masonite purchased at the hardware or lumber store.
- Glue sandpaper to your templates also. I usually make my templates from cardboard, but ask at your quilt shop for rough sided plastic template material.
- Place on the fabric and trace around the template. The line marked on the fabric is the sewing line. Cut ¼" seam allowance around each piece by eye.
- When sewing the pieces together, match the marked seam lines using pins. Sew on the marked line. After sewing the seam, check to make sure the stitches are on the lines, for both fabrics.

Templates Including Seam Allowance

You may want to use this method, especially if you have some sewing experience, but make sure to check the accuracy of your piecing. Your tie pieces might not go together as smoothly as the quilting cottons you are used to.

In this book, the seamlines on templates with seam allowance are marked - - - - -. The cutting lines are marked ———.

- Make your templates including ¼" seam allowance all around.
- Use a sandpaper board.
- Glue additional sandpaper to the reverse side of template.
- Place on the fabric and trace around the

template. Carefully cut on the marked line.

• When sewing the pieces together, match the edges and sew ¼" from the edges.

Making Templates from Paper Foundation Piecing Patterns

The instructions for some projects in this book are for piecing on paper foundations, but if you prefer to use templates, simply trace each pattern piece onto template material and add ¼" seam allowance, either onto the template, or cut the seam allowance by eye when cutting the fabric.

Using Templates On-Grain or Off-Grain

On most ties the stripes have diagonal designs (officially known as "regimental stripes") going across the wearer's chest. Most ties are cut on the diagonal because of the drape, but during the 50's, and one sees it again now, some ties are being cut on the straight of the grain.

The way you place your templates determines whether the piece is on-grain or off-grain. By thoughtful placement, you can enhance the diagonal beauty of the stripes and patterns. All the tie fabrics for my projects in this book, are cut off-grain.

The diagram (Fig. 1) shows how to place square and triangle templates on the tie fabric. The diagram shows a striped necktie to help you visualize the diagonal grain. (Of course, if you are using ties with no stripes or directional pattern, placement is not important.) Most striped ties have the stripes going in the direction as shown in Fig. 1 (remember, the example shows the reverse side of the tie).

The Shoo-Fly block in Fig. 2 is an example using triangles and square cut on-grain with background pieces also cut on-grain.

Rotary Cutting Pieces without Templates

The rotary cutter is a timesaving and helpful tool. Of course, you may use it to cut neckties. You

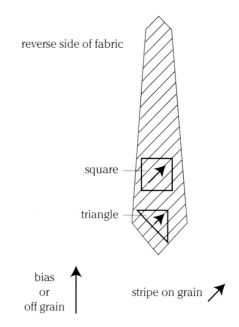

reverse side of fabric

square

triangle

bias or off grain

stripe on grain

Fig. 1

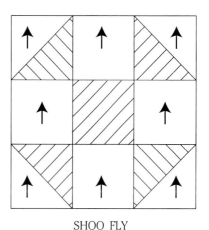

SHOO FLY

Fig. 2

OFF GRAIN

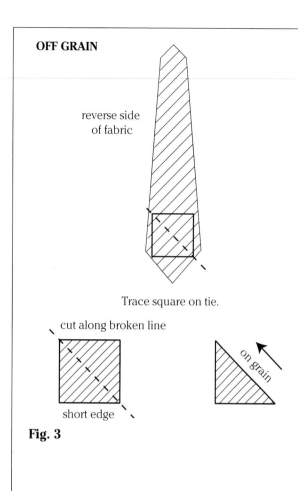

reverse side
of fabric

Trace square on tie.

cut along broken line

short edge

on grain

Fig. 3

OFF GRAIN

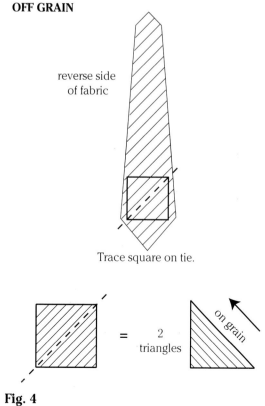

reverse side
of fabric

Trace square on tie.

= 2 triangles

on grain

Fig. 4

can use the rotary cutter with templates, or for cutting squares and half-square and quarter-square triangles without templates.

To prepare for rotary cutting, first stabilize part of each tie, fusing a piece of iron-on interfacing a little bigger than the area you need. Then stack four or five ties and cut without worrying about exactly lining up your template to cover each tie in the stabilized area. Don't worry about a little waste. In fact, save all your little scraps for Laura Mooers Woods' handbag, page 132. To cut a stack of ten, use flowerhead pins to prevent slipping and uneven cutting. Flowerhead pins are flat, allowing you to lay your ruler on top.

If you are making a quilt with right-angled triangles, you may want to try the half-square and quarter-square triangle technique. It is quicker than cutting individual templates.

With this technique, using a rotary cutter, you first cut a square and then cut it once diagonally to form two half-square triangles, or cut it twice diagonally to form four quarter-square triangles.

Your ties may not be wide enough to accommodate the size squares you need to cut half-square and quarter triangles. If so, cut triangles separately from templates.

Half-Square Triangles

To determine the size square to cut, measure the finished width of triangle (short side) and add 7/8" for seam allowance.

Example: 1½" finished triangle + 7/8" = 2⅜" square.

Cut one diagonal cut, creating two half-square triangles. The direction of the diagonal cut determines the grain orientation of the stripes. See Figs. 3 and 4 for cutting half-square triangles off-grain, with the stripes oriented in two different directions.

If you cut the squares on-grain, the half-square triangles will look like Figs. 5 and 6, again with the stripes going in two different directions depending on which way you make the diagonal cut.

Quarter-Square Triangles

To determine the size square to cut, measure the finished width of the triangle (long side) and add 1¼" for seam allowance.

Example: 1¾" finished triangle + 1¼" = 3" square.

Cut the square with two diagonal cuts to create four quarter-square triangles.

Keep in mind, when cutting quarter-square triangles, the results will be two triangles with vertical stripes and two triangles with horizontal stripes, all cut on-grain, if you position your square like Fig. 7.

To cut off-grain triangles, position your square and cut like Fig. 8, page 24.

Background Fabrics – On-Grain or Off-Grain

Some quilt patterns, such as Evening Star, page 30, have a "figure" which stands out from the background. For the quilts in this book, the figures (in this case, the star) are of tie fabrics. For the backgrounds, some of the quilts use tie fabrics and others use shirting, rayon, or more traditional quilting fabric.

In some patterns such as Shoo-Fly (Fig. 2, page 21), the background fabrics cut on the straight of the grain stitched together just fine to the particular ties I was using. This may not be the case for the ties and background fabrics you are using. If you find the pieces you are stitching difficult to handle or that they pucker after stitching, you may want to try cutting your background fabrics on the bias, in addition to the tie fabrics. Try the Shoo-Fly block, stitching bias to bias (Fig. 9, page 24).

When I made the quilt HAPPY FATHER'S DAY (page 14) and THESE TIES ARE FOR THE BIRDS (page 25), I purposely cut the shirting fabrics off-grain because I wanted the shirting fabric to integrate well in a horizontal/vertical pattern. By cutting on the diagonal, the striped shirting fabrics blended softly, letting the necktie fabrics be the center of attention. Fortunately, because of the 60°

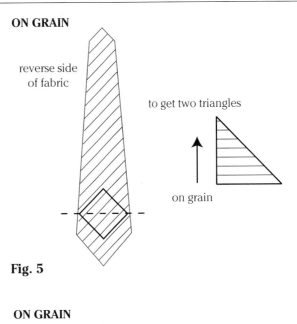

Fig. 5

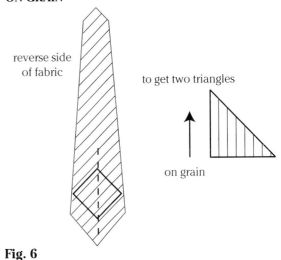

Fig. 6

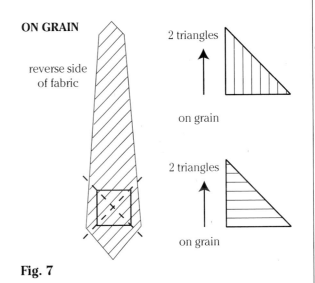

Fig. 7

ON GRAIN

reverse side
of fabric

2 triangles

2 triangles

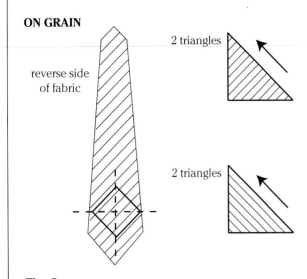

Fig. 8

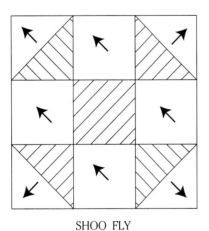

SHOO FLY

Fig. 9

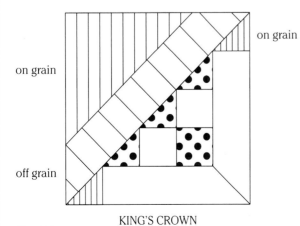

on grain

on grain

off grain

KING'S CROWN

Fig. 10

triangle design I had chosen, I was piecing bias to bias. Both quilts went together beautifully and the sides were plumb when finished.

Working with 45° squares and triangles presents new problems regarding whether to cut on-grain or off-grain. I like to keep the "tie look" which is off-grain. When I was preparing my fabrics for SCOTTY'S DILEMMA (page 56), I chose tartan wool neckties and several shades of solid yellow shirting fabrics. I cut everything off-grain because I thought the heavy wool ties would go together better this way. My tester block worked very nicely and the pieces fit together just fine.

Of course, the choice of grain line partly depends on the type of necktie fabrics you are using – polyester is sturdy, silk is wiggly – and also on the quality of the background material. Cottons are easy to use – there is no doubt about it – but I have used lots of rayon drapery samples and some softer fabrics which were more difficult to handle. I made them work – stabilizers are wonderful! There are solutions in this chapter that will solve your problems working with difficult fabrics.

In the King Crown Block, Fig. 10, some pieces are cut on-grain and some off-grain. With striped and patterned tie fabric, this variety of grainlines creates a unique look. You may have been taught to cut everything on the straight of the grain, both in making garments and quilts, but now is a good time to "break the rule" and see what interesting results you can create.

Sewing Techniques

Traditional

Necktie quilts can be pieced in the traditional manner, piecing individual pieces into units and then into sections, one at a time. This method may work well for you, especially if you have stabilized your tie fabric with interfacing. If using plastic template material, trace over patterns directly from the book.

THESE TIES ARE FOR THE BIRDS

67" x 67", by Janet B. Elwin, ©1992,
machine pieced and machine quilted, in the Elwin collection.

Foundation Methods

You may want to try a foundation method. Sewing to a fabric or paper foundation helps stabilize those stretchy slippery tie fabrics. Try this method for piecing lattice strips and some large background pieces, as well as blocks, for accuracy and to avoid stretching. Foundations are also very accurate, even for small pieces. The technique for

fabric and paper is the same, except that the paper is removed after the block is sewn and the fabric foundation remains.

In some cases you may need to use both interfacing and foundation piecing to stabilize a block, or perhaps one or the other will suffice.

Some blocks, such as the Log Cabin, Pineapple, and TIES IN THE SKY (page 77) can be pieced in a numbered sequence. Other blocks, such as Mariner's Compass are paper-pieced in sections which are then sewn together. Even though the sections need to be stitched together, the tie fabrics are still stabilized with this method.

Fabric Foundation Piecing

Log Cabin and crazy patchwork lend themselves very nicely to this technique. Jane Hall and Dixie Haywood call it "under pressed-piecing." Many of the old Log Cabin quilts were made with this method which is what I first taught my beginner students. The pattern is marked on a fabric foundation (usually muslin) and the pieces are stitched following a numbered sequence.

A disadvantage of using a fabric foundation is that hand quilting may be harder as you have to quilt through not only the tie fabrics, but also the muslin. For some projects I have found paper foundation (discussed later in this chapter) works better because you tear away the paper foundation and don't have the additional layer of fabric to deal with.

Crazy piecework in Eila Tegethoff's quilt, page 71, and other patterns can be pieced using this foundation method. You can use paper in place of fabric and fabric in place of paper for your foundation piecing.

Example of foundation piecing: Log Cabin block (see also the instructions for FREEDOM, page 122)

- Cut and mark, using a lightbox or carbon paper, a square of muslin the size of your block plus a ½" seam allowance around the outside edge.
- Using a rotary cutter, cut strips of fabric for each log ½" bigger all around than the finished piece. I add this extra seam allowance because somehow the fabric seems to shrink when doing foundation piecing.
- Stitch the fabrics to the wrong side of the muslin as follows:

‣ Hold the muslin up to the light with the marked side facing you so you can see what's happening on the other side of the fabric.

‣ Pin the center square of the Log Cabin, right side up, to cover the marked center square, leaving ½" all around. Pin the square to the side of the muslin which is *not* marked (Fig. 11).

‣ Holding the muslin up to the light, place the strip for log #1, right side down, over the center square. This strip is also placed on the unmarked side of the muslin (Fig. 12).

‣ On the marked side of the muslin, stitch along the marked seamline which joins the center square and log #1, extending the stitching three stitches beyond the marked line on each end.

‣ Trim the seam to ¼" if you wish. I don't hand quilt foundation pieced quilts, so unless there is an ungainly amount of fabric in the seam allowance, I don't trim along the seamline. Leave approximately ⅜" seam allowance at the end of each log.

‣ Flip log #1 so the right side is facing up and press the seam. It should cover the marked place on the pattern for log #1.

‣ Following the numbered sequence marked on the pattern, continue in this same manner until all the logs are stitched in place.

‣ Staystitch (baste) ¼" around the edge of the finished block to hold the fabric in place.

‣ Trim the finished block to size, including a ¼" seam allowance all around.

Paper Foundation Piecing

Paper foundation piecing is good to use when you plan to hand quilt because you will have less to quilt through with no stabilizer or foundation fabric. It is also a good method if you don't feel the ties need a stabilizer but they have a bit of give that you would like to control. This method is very accurate and even when the papers are removed, the blocks hold their shape. When cutting fabric pieces for this method, I cut, by eye, around all sides ½" larger than the finished size. This gives a little extra for shrinkage in sewing and an extra bit of seam allowance so when removing papers. The seams don't fray.

I like this technique so well that most of the patterns in this book use it. Let's face it – working with ties is a challenge. I have found the paper foundation method a great help in making life easier and my quilts looking really good.

Preparing Paper Patterns

You can duplicate the paper patterns directly from this book. If you are uneasy about photocopying directly from a book, put a piece of tracing paper over the pattern and copy it using a ruler and black pen. When putting tracing paper in the photocopy machine, put a piece of plain white paper on top. The copy will come out nice and clear.

Check the first copy against the original in the book. It should be the same. Make as many copies as you need for blocks in the quilt. If you find that the block has been distorted when photocopying, try making needle-punched papers as described on page 28. This method of transferring the pattern is very accurate.

The Mariner's Compass pattern is divided into sections. Follow the directions for paper piecing each section. Sew the sections together in numbered sequence to complete the block. See Mariner's Compass, page 46.

Making Needle-Punched Papers

I prefer Pellon® Stitch-N-Tear® to regular paper because it is lightweight but sturdy.

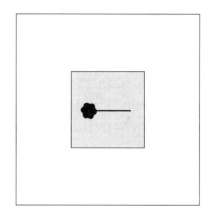

Fig. 11

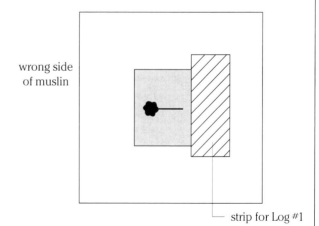

wrong side of muslin

strip for Log #1

Fig. 12

- Cut a piece of Pellon® Stitch-N-Tear® about ½" bigger all around the entire block pattern or around the section if the block will be foundation pieced in sections.
- Draw the pattern or sections onto Stitch-N-Tear®.
- Place the drawn pattern on top of the Stitch-N-Tear®. To make multiple blocks, needle-punch six papers at a time. Pile up six pieces of Stitch-N-Tear® and staple the edges so they stay together.
- Unthread the sewing machine needle and remove the bobbin.
- Machine "stitch" (needle-punch) using a long stitch length, perforating along the drawn lines.
- Remove the staples and separate the papers.

It isn't necessary to transfer the numbers and/or letters onto every piece of paper. Once you have done one, you will remember the sequence.

Sewing Paper Foundation Piecing

Paper foundation piecing is sewn the same way as foundation piecing onto a fabric foundation, except that with paper foundation piecing, the papers are removed at the end. See the instructions for sewing fabric foundation piecing for piecing an entire block (Log Cabin example) and for a block pieced in sections (Mariner's Compass, page 46).

No yardage requirements are given for the Pellon® stabilizers or paper as I can't predict how much you would want or need to use.

Brief instructions are given for finishing each project in this book, including pressing, basting the quilt top to the batting and backing, quilting, and binding. I often quilt traditionally, ¼" in along all the seams. I usually keep my quilting pretty simple, but sometimes have used my fancy sewing machine stitches. When I do this, I will tell you the stitch setting (on the Pfaff Creative 7550 sewing machine).

It is up to you to decide whether to hand or machine quilt. My necktie quilts are all machine quilted because of the fabric content – lots of polyester and some quilts with muslin foundations. Make these quilt projects your own by quilting using your favorite method(s).

All my quilts have been bound using neckties also. Some of the smaller projects require only one tie, but if you need more, just select compatible ties to enhance your quilt. It makes an interesting binding when you use a variety of ties. I cut the binding 1½" wide and stitch it to the quilt. Then fold it to the back of the quilt and turn under the edge and hand hem in place.

Try the methods in this chapter and see what works best for you and the types of ties you are working with.

The technique which I have found most successful for the majority of piecing with neckties is to stabilize the lightweight neckties and then to sew them to Pellon® Stitch-N-Tear® foundations. This is a win-win situation, especially when piecing some of the more complicated patterns.

I recommend that beginners take the extra steps of ironing on interfacing and using needle-punched papers to get excellent results. Try this technique at least once. See how you like the finished sharp lines.

For each project in this book, I experimented, trying to come up with the best, quickest, most accurate, and easiest method to achieve great looking pieced blocks.

Chapter

3

Some Great Patterns

The quilts in the chapter are easy and suitable
for all levels of quiltmaking skills.

CYNTHIA STAR

67" x 67", by Janet B. Elwin, ©1994,
machine pieced and machine quilted, in the Elwin collection.

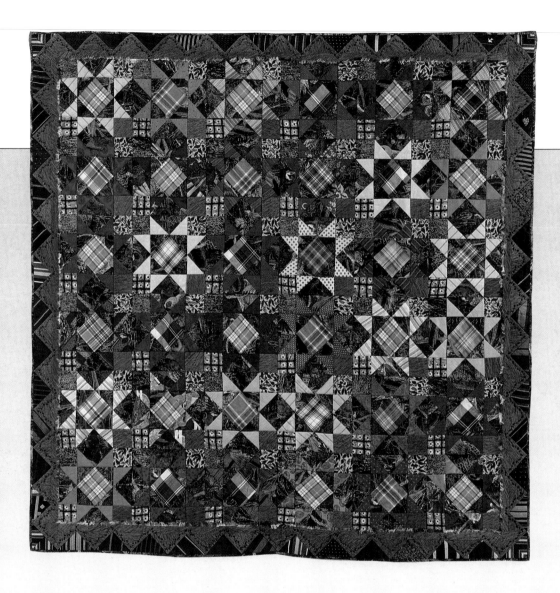

Into our lives the most extraordinary people come and go. In my life, one of those was my friend Cynthia Tobey. I am sometimes overwhelmed when I think of her quiet influence on her family and friends. This quilt is dedicated to her.

This quilt, from a very easy block called Evening Star, has 36 blocks with repeated fabrics in each, except for the 36 different neckties and the center square plaids. Using these different fabrics makes a simple pattern look rich and complex.

The combination of the fabrics in this quilt is eclectic. There are two African prints, two Marimekko fabrics from Finland, and a black print called "Jewel of the Jungle" by Hoffman of California. The Hoffman print is taken from a dress I had for years. The center square plaids were fringed cocktail napkins bought at a yard sale. While trimming the cocktail napkins to size I decided to keep the fringed edge and add it along the border. The fringe adds a little spunk. There are great plaids available that can be used in place of my cocktail napkins. You can have a lot of fun choosing your own interesting fabrics for this quilt.

Techniques
Templates
Half-square and quarter-square triangles
All fabrics cut on-grain except for ties

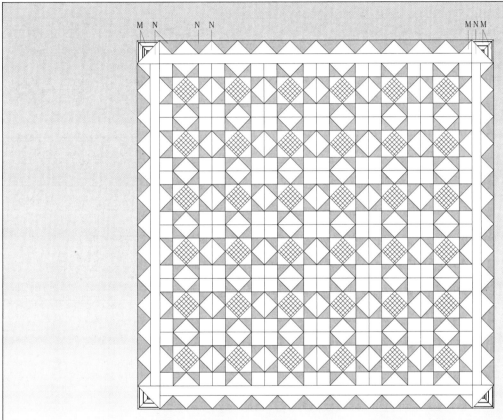

CYNTHIA STAR

Because this quilt was made mostly with good cotton fabric and just the star was made from ties, the pieces were rotary cut. If your fabric choices are like mine, this may be a good opportunity to try cutting quarter-square triangles (see Chapter 2).

Preparing Fabric for Rotary Cutting
- Fold the washed fabric, right sides together, with the selvage edges together.
- Iron the fabric.
- Fold the fabric again. Fold in half again so the selvages meet.

- Iron the four layers together. The steam from the iron helps keep the layers together. This is the optimum number of layers I like to cut at one time.

FOR THE TEMPLATE METHOD:

Fabric (all cotton except ties)	# of Ties	Yardage	Template	# to Cut
Neckties	36		M	8 each
Squares, 4 coordinating		⅜ yard	L	36 each
Black print		2½ yards	M	144
			N	144
Plaid		½ yard	O	36
Red for highlighter		¾ yard		4 strips 1½" x 60½"*
Red for triangle border (use same red as for the highlighter)			M	8
			N	48
Black ties for border	12		N	4 each
	1		M	8
Backing		4 yards		
Binding from black print				

* Includes seam allowance.

FOR THE QUARTER-SQUARE TRIANGLE METHOD for NON-STRIPED TIES
(The yardage requirements for the non-tie fabrics are the same as for the template method.)

Fabric	# of Ties	# to Cut	Squares	# to Cut	Quarter Squares*
4 coordinated squares		36 each	3"		
Ties	36			2 each	4¾"
Black print				36	4¾"
				36	6¼"
Plaid center		36	4"		
Red				11	6¼"
				2	4¾"
Black ties	12			1 each	6¼"
Black ties for corners	1			2	4¾"

Red border: Cut 4 highlighter strips 1½" x 60½".
* Includes seam allowance.

The quarter-square triangle method works well with plain and patterned ties (see chart on previous page). However, after cutting quarter-square triangles from striped ties, all the stripes will not be going in the same direction. If the majority of your ties are striped and you wish to cut them with the stripe going in the same direction, use half-square triangles and cut according to the following chart.

FOR THE HALF-SQUARE AND QUARTER-SQUARE TRIANGLE METHOD FOR STRIPED TIES
(The yardage requirements for the non-tie fabrics are the same as for the template method.)

Fabric	# of Ties	# to Cut	Squares	# to Cut	Half-Squares	# to Cut	Quarter-Squares*
4 coordinated squares			36 each	3"			
Ties for blocks	36			4 each	3⅜"		
Black print						36	4¾"
						36	6¼"
Plaid center		36	4"				
Red						11	6¼"
						2	4¾"
Black ties	12			2 each	4⅜"		
Black tie for corners	1			4	3⅜"		

Border: Cut 4 highlighter strips 1½" x 60½".
* Includes seam allowance.

Assembly

• Put together each Evening Star block according to the diagram (Fig. 13).
• Press each block.
• Arrange the blocks in a grouping which you like – 6 across by 6 down.
• Stitch them together in rows.

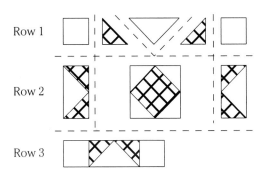

Row 1

Row 2

Row 3

Fig. 13

Fig. 14

Fig. 15

Fig. 16

Highlighter and Triangle Borders

The Evening Star blocks are bordered by a highlighter strip (which is something like an inner mat on a framed picture) and an outer border of triangles. Assemble them according to the diagrams.

- Stitch 12 triangles (N) from different black ties and 11 red triangles (N) into a strip, adding red half triangles (piece M) at each end (Fig. 14).
- Add the highlighter strips (Fig. 15).
- Stitch triangles for the top and bottom borders in the same sequence as Step 1 (Fig. 14).
- Add the highlighter strips and red triangles (N) to each end (Fig. 16).
- Stitch the side borders and then the top and bottom borders to the quilt top (Fig. 17).
- Add the black triangles (M) to the outer corners (Fig. 18).

Finishing

- Press the finished quilt top.
- Baste the quilt top to the batting and backing.
- Quilt ¼" in from the seams in all the pieces.
- Bind the quilt with the black print.

Fig. 17

Fig. 18

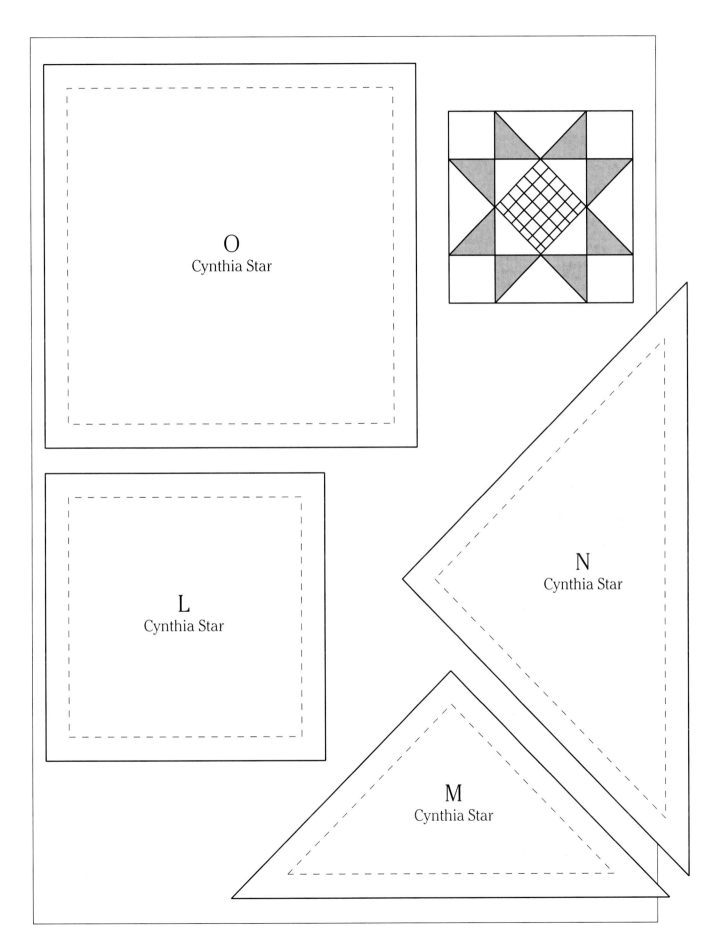

O
Cynthia Star

L
Cynthia Star

N
Cynthia Star

M
Cynthia Star

TAILSPIN – TIESPIN

33" x 33", by Norma Schlager, ©1995,
machine pieced and machine quilted.

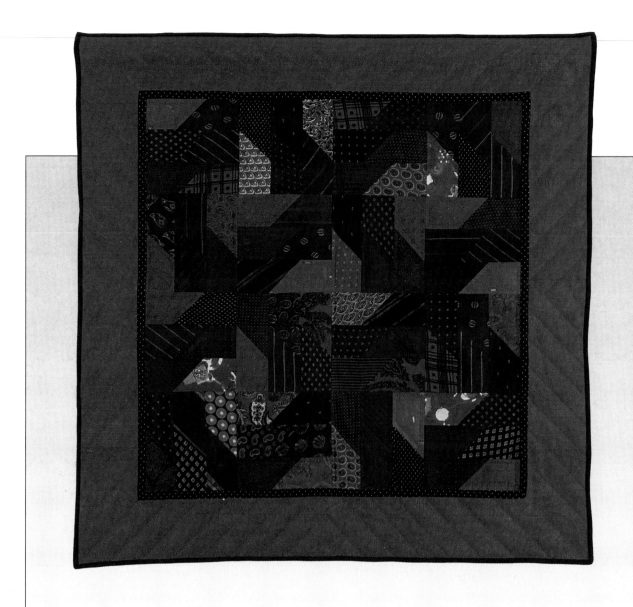

Norma makes beautiful crazy quilt vests from neckties and wanted to try a quilt project. She saw a Friendship Star variation called Picket Fence in *Quiltmaker* magazine. Working with the slippery silk ties drove her crazy until she incorporated Pellon®. Those of you familiar with this pattern may not recognize Norma's version. After she finished the quilt, she called me in a dither because she had used the templates in reverse – mirror image.

But, she really likes the new version and you will too. At the end of these directions, a drawing of the original block will show you how, if you reverse the templates, you can have two separate blocks using this one pattern.

Techniques

Templates

Half-square and quarter-square triangles

All fabrics cut on-grain except for ties

TAILSPIN – TIESPIN

FOR THE TAILSPIN – TIESPIN QUILT

Section of Quilt	Fabric	# of Ties	Yardage	Template	# to Cut
Blocks	Red ties	6		A	32 pieces
Blocks	Charcoal, navy, and black ties	4 each		A	64 pieces total from darks
Highlighter	Black microdot silk		¼ yard strips 1" x 33½"*		4
Border	Red silk		½ yard strips 4½" x 33½"*		4
Backing	Muslin		1yard		
Binding	Black**				

* Includes seam allowance.

**Norma used Coupe De Ville (polyester) backed with interfacing, but you can use fabric of your choice.

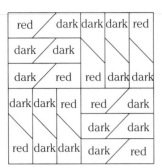

Fig. 19

Fig. 20

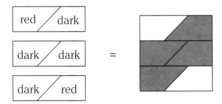

Fig. 21

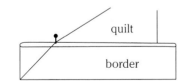

Fig. 22

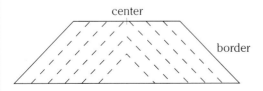

Fig. 23

Instructions

The quilt is made from four 12" blocks. Cut all the pieces and lay out the colors according to the diagram which is for one 12" block (Fig. 19).

Stitching Sequence

- Stitch each red/dark unit together (Fig. 20).
- Stitch each quarter block together (Fig. 21).
- Press.
- Arrange each quarter block according to the diagram and stitch together in rows (Fig. 19).

Border

- Stitch the highlighter strips to the red border strips.
- Press seams.
- Miter the corners as follows:
  ‣ Measure in 5" and mark on each end of all four border strips.
  ‣ Pin the borders to the edges of the quilt. Stitch ¼" in from the edge of the quilt and end stitching ¼" from the edge.
  ‣ Repeat for the remaining three borders.
  ‣ Fold two borders at a corner of the quilt so they lay parallel to each other. Draw a line, using a pencil and ruler, from the stitched edge of quilt to the outer corner of the border (Fig. 22).
  ‣ Stitch the corner seam from the quilt edge to the outer border.
  ‣ After checking to make sure it has been stitched accurately, trim the seam allowance to ¼".

Finishing

- Press the finished quilt top.
- Baste the quilt top to the batting and backing.
- Quilt ¼" in around each piece. Quilt diagonal lines 1¼" apart in the border (Fig. 23).
- Bind the quilt with black fabric.

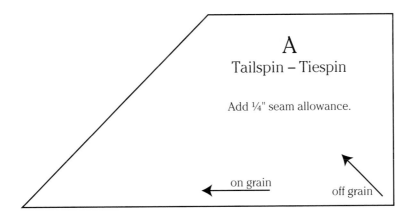

A
Tailspin – Tiespin

Add ¼" seam allowance.

on grain

off grain

NECKTIE GEMINI

23" x 23", by Rhoda Cohen, c.1994,
machine pieced and hand quilted.

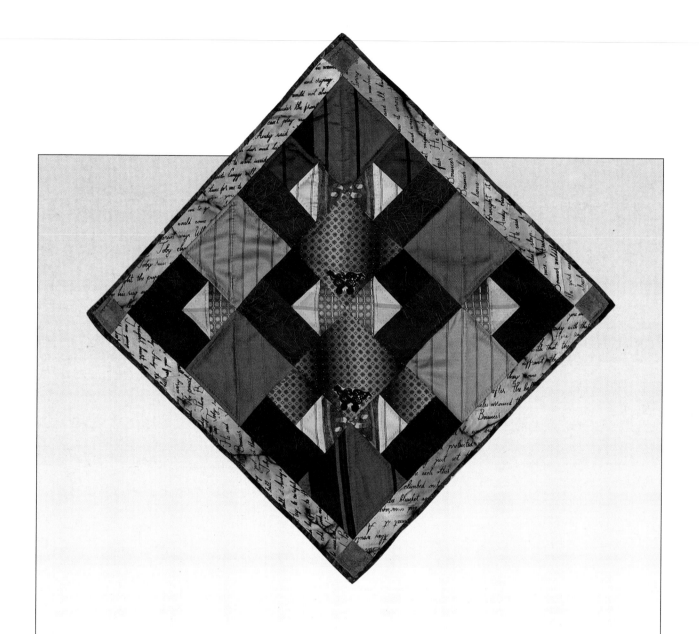

Rhoda really doesn't collect neckties. She did this particular project by selecting fabrics from a sample packet of ties given her by a friend connected with the tie trade. She likes the fact that ties emphasize the dynamic of diagonal design and the light reflective properties of the silk. Rhoda notes these fabrics are usually malleable while holding their shapes. Necktie Gemini evolved through the piecing accomplished by pairing elements: triangle to triangle to form squares, then squares to squares forming rectangles, rectangle to rectangle, etc.

Techniques

Templates, no seam allowance
Traditional piecing

FOR THE NECKTIE GEMINI QUILT

Section of Quilt	Fabric	# of Ties	Yardage	Template	# to Cut
Blocks	Blue stripe ties	1		A	2
				D	2
	Beige/red stripe tie	1		A	2
	Taupe/pink stripe tie	1		A	2
	Blue/blue print tie	1		A	2
				D	2
	Copper leaf print tie	1		B	4
				D	4
	Yellow/green stripe tie	1		C	4
	Brown/pink print tie	1		C	4
	Yellow/print stripe tie	1		C	4
	Gray-green print tie	1		C	4
	Copper line print tie	1		B	4
	Pink/gold border tie	1		E	4
Border	Print tie	1	2" x 20½" strip*		4
Backing			⅝ yard		
Binding	Tie	1			

* Measurement includes seam allowance.

Stitching Sequence

Refer to the outlined area in the diagram Fig. 25, page 42, to make a set.

- Stitch the triangle sets together first (piece #6 to #7) (Fig. 24).
- Press all the seams open.

Fig. 24

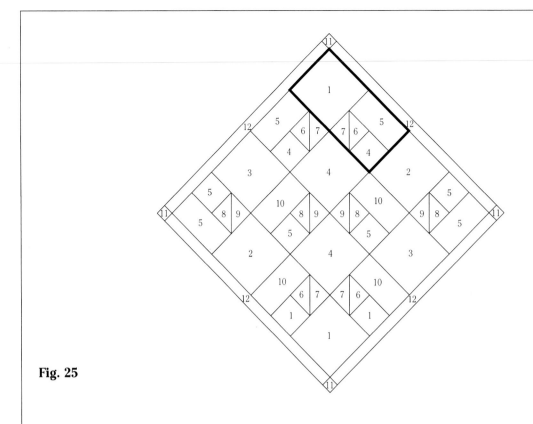

Fig. 25

Fig. 26   **Fig. 27**

Fig. 28

Fig. 29

- Stitch the triangle set (#6 and #7) to a square (#4), creating a pieced rectangle (Fig. 26).
- Stitch the pieced rectangle to piece #5, creating a pieced square (Fig. 27).
- Stitch the pieced square to piece #1, creating one set (Fig. 28).
- Repeat to make seven more sets following the numbered diagram.
- Layout each set on a flannel board.
- Stitch the sets together in rows as shown below. The numbers in each set coincide with the numbers in the diagram below (Fig. 29).

Border

- Stitch two border strips (#12) to each side of the assembled blocks.
- Stitch the squares (#11) to each side of the remaining two border strips (#12) for the

top and bottom (Fig. 30).

- Stitch these borders to the top and bottom of the quilt (Fig. 31).

Finishing

- Press the finished quilt top.
- Baste the quilt top to the batting and backing.
- Rhoda quilted ¼" away from the seams on all the shapes. On the border she quilted diagonal lines about 1¾" apart. She also appliquéd Gemini (twin) fabric on the blue/blue fabric (piece #4).
- Hang the quilt on the diagonal. Sew this special sleeve as follows. Cut a triangle of backing fabric with the short sides of the triangle the length of the quilt plus seam allowance (Fig. 32).

  Baste the large triangle onto the back of the quilt as shown (Fig. 33).

  Cut mat board (can be found at art supply stores) or other sturdy material to fit into the triangular sleeve. Poke a hole through the top of the mat board triangle with a compass point. Insert the mat board into the sleeve. Nail a 1" finishing nail in the wall. Hang the quilt.

Fig. 30

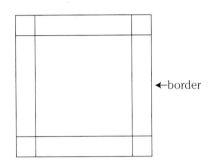

Fig. 31

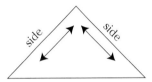

Fig. 32

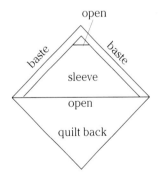

Fig. 33

E
for border
Necktie Gemini

B
Necktie Gemini

D
Necktie Gemini

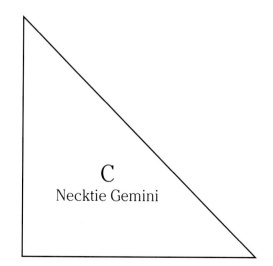

C
Necktie Gemini

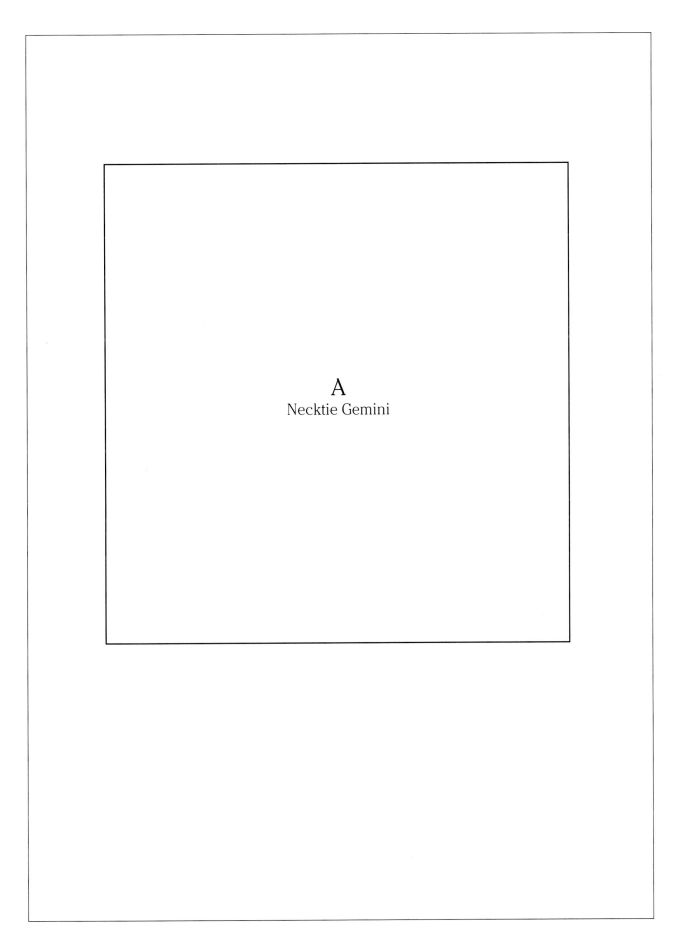

A
Necktie Gemini

MARINER'S COMPASS

40½" x 40½", *by Janet B. Elwin,* ©1995,
machine pieced and machine quilted, in the Elwin collection.

Now that you have tried some of the techniques and have figured out which of your fabrics need special attention, this quilt may be just the project for you. The quilt is a small wallhanging size. Don't be put off by this beautiful design. I used to give my beginner quilters a Mariner's Compass to do as a side project. They loved it and found if you follow the instructions step-by-step, this isn't difficult at all.

Techniques

Paper foundation piecing
Appliqué
Blended inner border

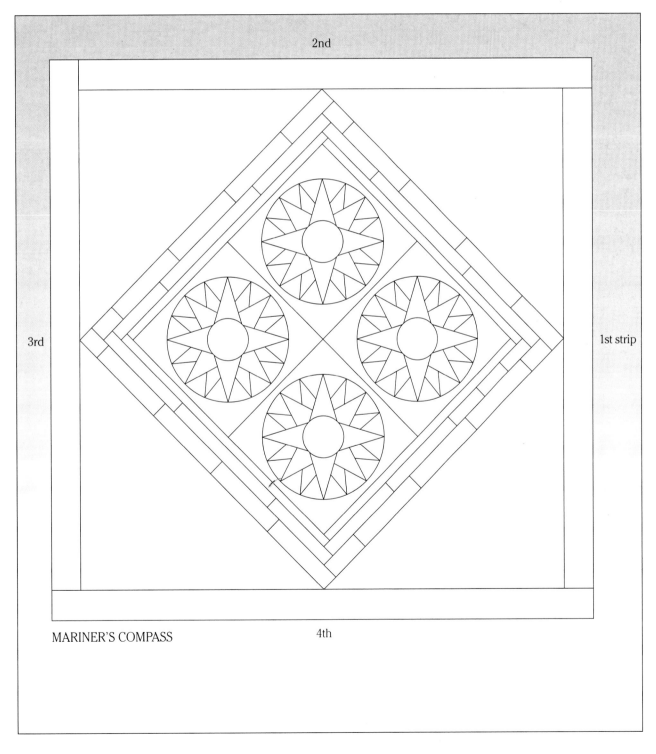

2nd

3rd

1st strip

MARINER'S COMPASS

4th

FOR THE MARINER'S COMPASS

Section of Quilt	Fabric	# of Ties	Yardage
Compasses	Dark tie	1	
	Medium tie	1	
	Light tie	1	
Center circles	Wine tie	1	
Background	Blended (closely related in value) fabrics		16 pieces – 1½" x 3"
	OR solid color cotton		1 yard
Highlighter	Striped tie	1	
Inner border	Ties, a variety of coordinating	4	14 strips – 4" x 8"
Outer border	Ties, a variety of coordinating	4	4 strips 3" x 38½"
Large triangles	Solid color cotton*		⅝ yard
Backing			1 yard
Binding	Tie	2	
Stick-N-Tear®			2 yards

* You can use the same fabric for both the background and the large triangles (1⅝ yards for both).

Preparation

- Cut papers in rectangle shapes as in the diagram Fig. 34.
- Needle-punch papers as follows:
  - ▸ 32 copies of E-D-E
  - ▸ 16 copies of C
  - ▸ 16 copies of B
  - ▸ 4 copies of A
  - ▸ 16 copies of the background piece
- If using 16 blended fabrics for the background, number the papers (E-D-E) in the margin 1 through 16 to indicate where the different colors will go (Fig. 34).

  If using one fabric for the background, disregard this instruction.

Assembly of Compasses

- Cut a 1½" x 3" rectangle of light tie fabric and pin to cover D. I found it easier to cut rectangles for this piece even though the

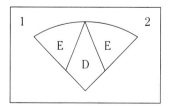

Fig. 34

piece is diamond-shaped.

- Cut 2 E pieces from Fabric 1 and 2. For these pieces and all the rest, cut by eye ½" larger than the finished section.

- Position Fabric 1 and stitch along the seamline. Trim the fabric along the stitched seam to ¼". Iron. Repeat for Fabric 2 (Fig. 35).

- Staystitch along the needle-punched lines as they will be your sewing lines when you assemble the project.

- Repeat for the remaining seven E-D-E sections in the first compass.

- If you are using a blended background, set the papers aside at this point. Don't trim them, as you will eliminate the numbers which will be helpful if your colors are very close. If you are using a same color background, after staystitching, trim to ¼" and set aside.

- Cut a piece from the medium necktie and pin to paper C. Staystitch. Trim to ¼" all around, leaving the papers in place (Fig. 36).

- Cut a piece from the dark necktie and pin to paper B. Staystitch and trim as above.

- Repeat the above 2 steps to prepare the additional pieces B and C for the 15 sections needed for the four compasses.

- Lay out all the compass background pieces in the correct numbered sequence. At this point, trim blended E-D-E pieces.

- Stitch the units along staystitching lines in the following sequence:
    - Fabric 1 – 2 to left of piece C. Iron.
    - Fabric 2 – 3 to right of piece C. Iron (Fig. 37).

- Repeat for the remaining units in all the compasses.

- Stitch the above unit E-D-E-C-E-D-E to piece B. Iron the seam away from B (Fig. 38).

- Repeat for the remaining units in all the compasses.

- Carefully remove the papers.

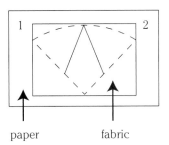

paper   fabric

Fig. 35

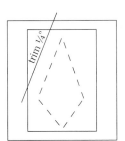

Fig. 36

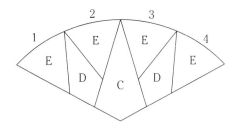

Right side of fabrics

Fig. 37

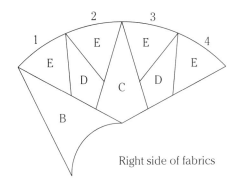

Right side of fabrics

Fig. 38

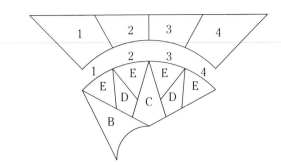

Fig. 39

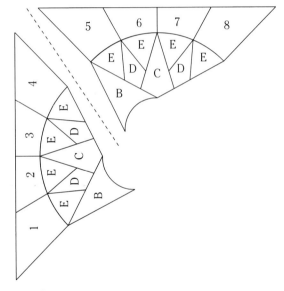

Fig. 40

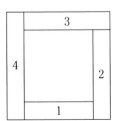

Fig. 41

Pieced Background Around the Outside of the Compass

- Cut the background papers in rectangles and number them to coordinate with colors 1 – 16.
- As before, cut each fabric piece ½" larger than the finished section.
- Stitch the fabrics following the numbered sequence for all the background sections. Staystitch. Iron.
- Arrange the background sections to match the adjacent E-D-E fabrics.
- Trim the background sections leaving ¼" seam allowance.
- Remove the papers.
- Pin the background sections to the B-C-D units and stitch along staystitching lines. This makes a quarter section of a compass block. *Do not* stitch beyond these lines (Fig. 39).
- Repeat for the remaining sections in all the compasses.
- Pin and stitch the three remaining quarter sections of the compass block along the staystitching. Iron the seams to the left. Repeat, completing all four compass blocks (Fig. 40).
- Baste the center circle to a paper circle. Trim to ¼". Hand appliqué to the center of the compass, turning under the edges. Or baste the circle to paper and machine appliqué using a buttonhole stitch (#12 on the Pfaff Creative 7550).
- Stitch the four compass blocks together, two by two.

Highlighter Strip

- Cut one strip of tie fabric ⅞" x 80".
- Stitch the highlighter strips along the quilt top as you would a Log Cabin block, adding each strip in the numbered sequence shown in the diagram below (Fig. 41).

Inner Borders - 2 rows

Because I was using drapery samples, my pieces were limited by size. Feel free to make changes to these instructions. I used 4" x 5" and 4" x 8" pieces.

- Piece together fabrics, complementary to your compasses, to make a border strip 4" x 106". Iron. Cut the strip as shown, creating one strip 1½" x 106" for the first inner border and one strip 2½" x 106" for the second inner border (Fig. 42).
- Stitch the first inner border (1½" strips) to the quilt top Log Cabin style as shown below. Iron (Fig. 43).
- For the second border (2½" strips), cut off 5" from the beginning of the length and add the piece to the end to change the color position of the pieces (Fig. 44).
- Stitch the second border on as in the second step above (Fig. 45).

At This Point You Can End Your Quilt

But, if you would like a larger variation, continue on…

Corner Triangles

- Cut two 18⅝" squares. Cut in half to make four half-square triangles.
- Mark the center of each triangle and the center of the border. Pin at the center and along the edge.
- Sew one triangle to each border.

Outer Border

- Cut four ties 3" x 38½".
- Measure in 6¼" on the first border. Pin in 4" on the triangle. Stitch the border to the quilt, matching up the pins. Start stitching at the pins and sew to the opposite edge of the quilt.
- Stitch the second border strip, covering the end of the first strip and sewing to the edge

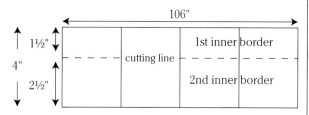

Fig. 42

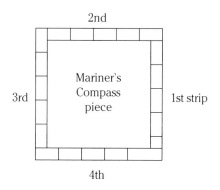

stitched Log Cabin Style

Fig. 43

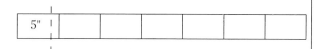

Fig. 44

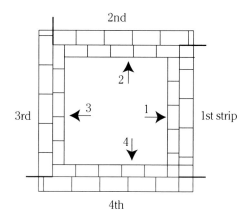

stitched Log Cabin Style

Fig. 45

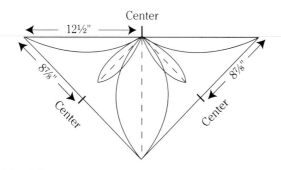

Fig. 46

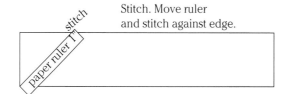

Fig. 47

of the quilt. Repeat for the remaining border strips.

- Remove the pin from first border. Finish sewing the seam for the first border to the edge of the quilt, covering the end of the fourth border.

Finishing

- Press the finished quilt top.
- Baste the quilt top to the batting and backing.
- Quilt in-the-ditch on the compasses and highlighter strip. I used Pfaff stitch #203 along the inner border.

Quilt oval shapes in the large corner triangles as follows. Make paper templates for the large and small ovals. Pin the large oval template to the centerline of the large triangle. Machine quilt along the edge of the oval. Move the centerline of the large oval to the inner border seam and quilt around the template in the triangle area. Quilt the small ovals to fit between the large ones. After you have quilted the large and small ovals, echo quilt ⅜" in as many times as will fit inside the ovals (Fig. 46).

With a paper ruler, quilt diagonal lines at 1" intervals along the borders. To do this without marking your quilt, make a sturdy paper template approximately 1" x 10". Line up the strip of paper at an angle. Hold the paper in position and stitch against the edge of the paper. Reposition your ruler and stitch the next line until border is quilted in diagonal lines.

This is a great way to quilt without marking. On other quilts I have used this same technique and simply varied the sizes of my paper ruler (Fig. 47).

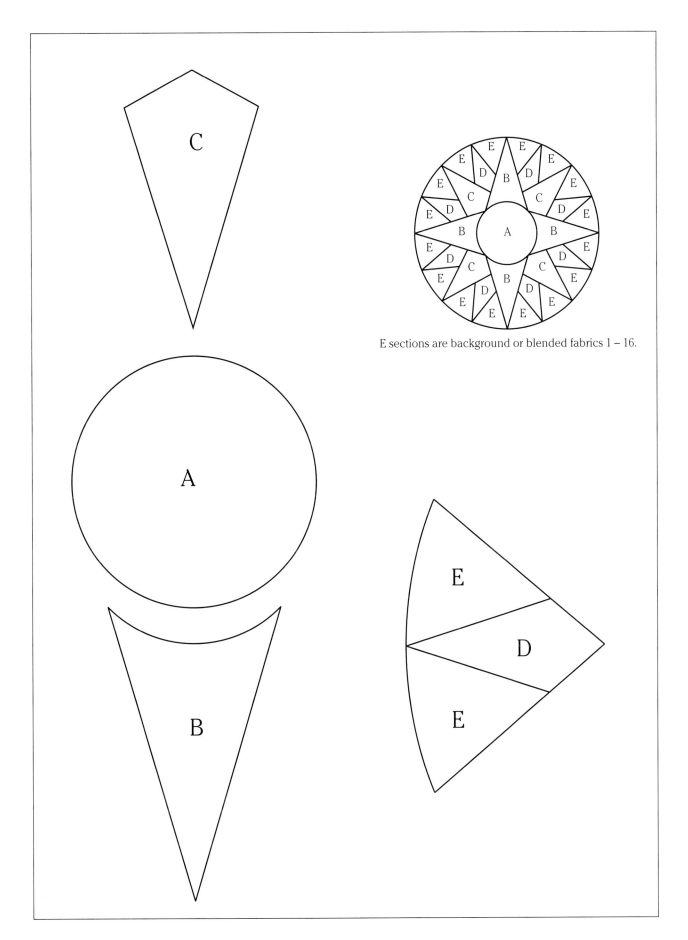

E sections are background or blended fabrics 1 – 16.

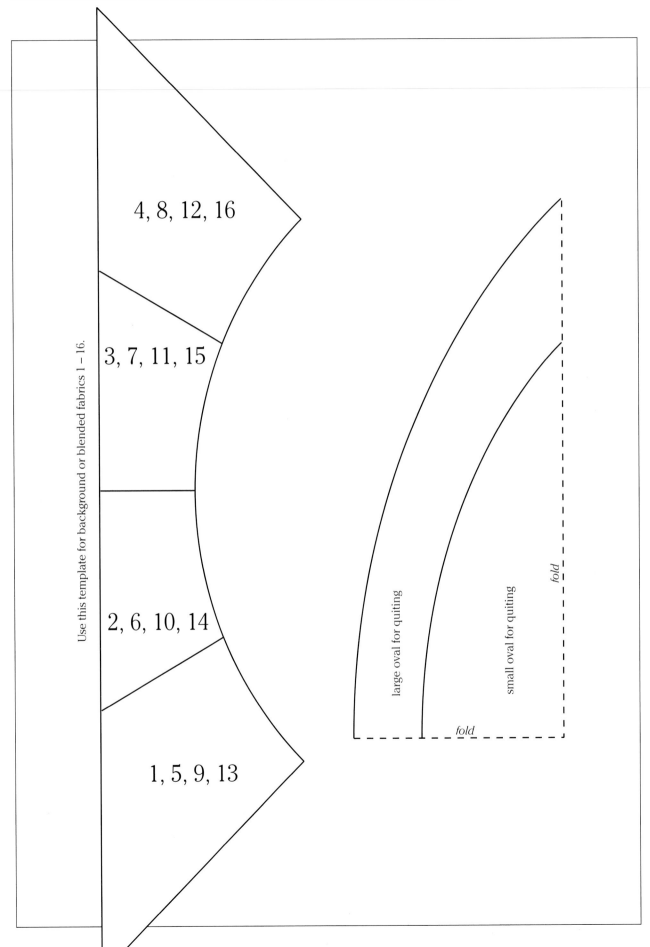

Use this template for background or blended fabrics 1 – 16.

4, 8, 12, 16

3, 7, 11, 15

2, 6, 10, 14

1, 5, 9, 13

large oval for quiting

small oval for quiting

fold

fold

SCOTTY'S DILEMMA

40" x 40", by Janet B. Elwin, ©1994,
machine pieced and machine quilted, in the Elwin collection.

During a trip to Scotland and England in 1993, I had an opportunity to add to the couple of tartan ties in my collection. I scoured charity shops and discovered that Scottish men really hold on to their tartan ties. They probably pass them down from father to son. I did manage to find a few, but Pam Fairless in Peebles, Scotland, added to my bounty by giving me five pieces of tartan fabrics used to make ties.

The name for this quilt was inspired by this story told to me by Marie Telfer about her father. During World War II, Joseph Ayre of Scotland was a musician in the Royal Air Force. As the war was ending, Joe traveled from country to country with the band for all the peace treaty signings. On an American ship that carried a large contingent of Canadians and Americans, Joe was the only Scotsman on board, as well as the only band member.

They nicknamed him "Scotty." Scotty's dilemma was being "encouraged" to entertain the troops every evening until the wee hours of the morning. He just couldn't say "no" because the men had been through so much. When they reached their destination, the troops marched off the ship with the regiments, the smallest regiment first. Joe was the only member of this group present and the first to march off the ship. The soldiers on board gave him a standing ovation, clapping and cheering to show their appreciation of his talents. What a send-off for Scotty!

My dilemma was what to do next when I had finished the Aunt Sukey's Choice blocks and wasn't happy with them. My happy solution was to combine the Aunt Sukey's Choice blocks with Nine-Patch blocks, set on point with a narrow border. The combination of these two blocks gives an updated twist to two old patterns.

FOR THE SCOTTY'S DILEMMA QUILT

Fabric	# of Ties	Yardage	Template	# to Cut
Aunt Sukey Block – tartan ties	16		A	4 each from 8 ties
			D	1 each from 8 ties
to coordinate with A and D			C and CR	4 each from 8 ties
Yellow shirting #1, #2, #3		⅛ yard each	A	32 each
Yellow shirting #4		¼ yard	B	64 each
Yellow shirting #5, #6		⅛ yard each	B	32 each
Nine-Patch Block – tartan ties (same as above)	16		E	5 each from 8 ties
to coordinate with tartan ties above			E	4 each
			G	4 each from 8 ties
Yellow shirting #7, #8		⅛ yard each	F	32 each

I cut all shirting, plain, striped, and checked fabrics off-grain. I did not use PELLON® on wool.

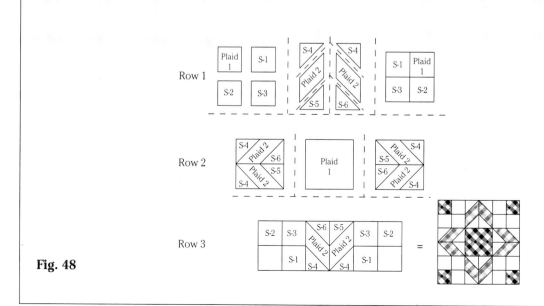

Fig. 48

Techniques

Templates

Traditional piecing

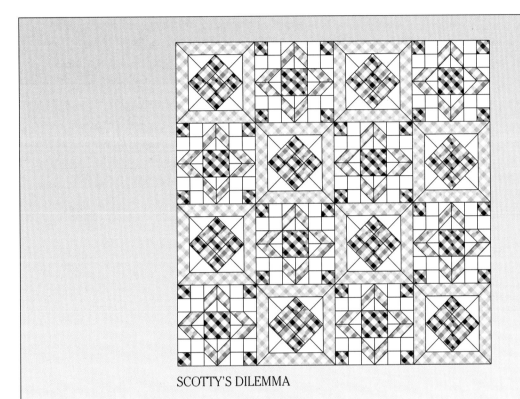

SCOTTY'S DILEMMA

Stitching Sequence

Aunt Sukey's Block

Make eight blocks as shown in Fig. 48, page 56.
Press.

Nine-Patch Block

Make eight blocks as shown in Fig. 49. Press.

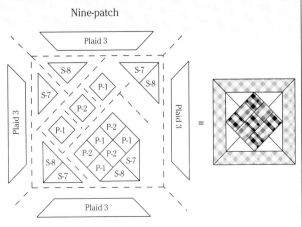

Fig. 49

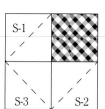

Fig. 50

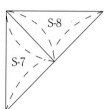

Fig. 51

Quilt Assembly

Lay out the blocks, four across by four down, alternating the Aunt Sukey blocks with the Nine-Patches. Stitch the blocks together.

Finishing

- Press the finished quilt top.
- Baste the quilt top to the batting and backing.
- Quilt the Aunt Sukey blocks in-the-ditch except on shirting fabrics #1, #2, #3. On those quilt diagonally through the centers Fig. 50.

For the Nine-Patch blocks, trace the rose quilting design onto eight papers. Pin in the centers of the Nine-Patch blocks. Quilt and remove the papers. For shirting fabrics #7 and #8, make a template from the melon-shaped quilting design. Hold it in place with the centerline over the seams and quilt around the template Fig. 51.

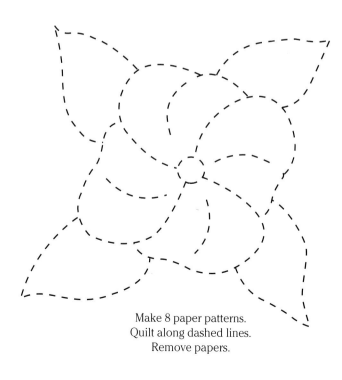

Make 8 paper patterns.
Quilt along dashed lines.
Remove papers.

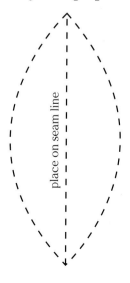

Make paper pattern and
quilt along edge.

place on seam line

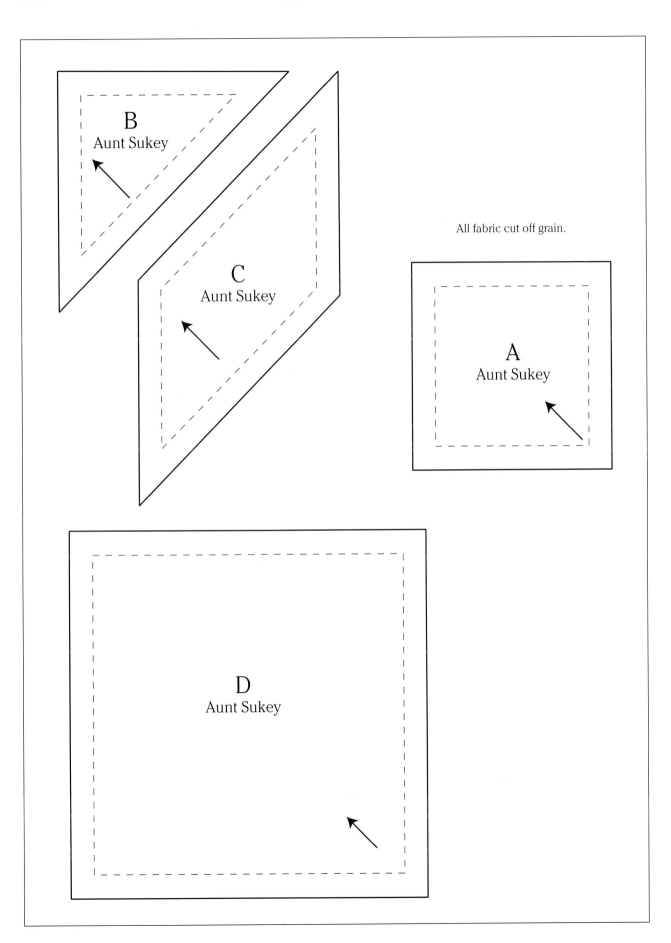

B
Aunt Sukey

C
Aunt Sukey

All fabric cut off grain.

A
Aunt Sukey

D
Aunt Sukey

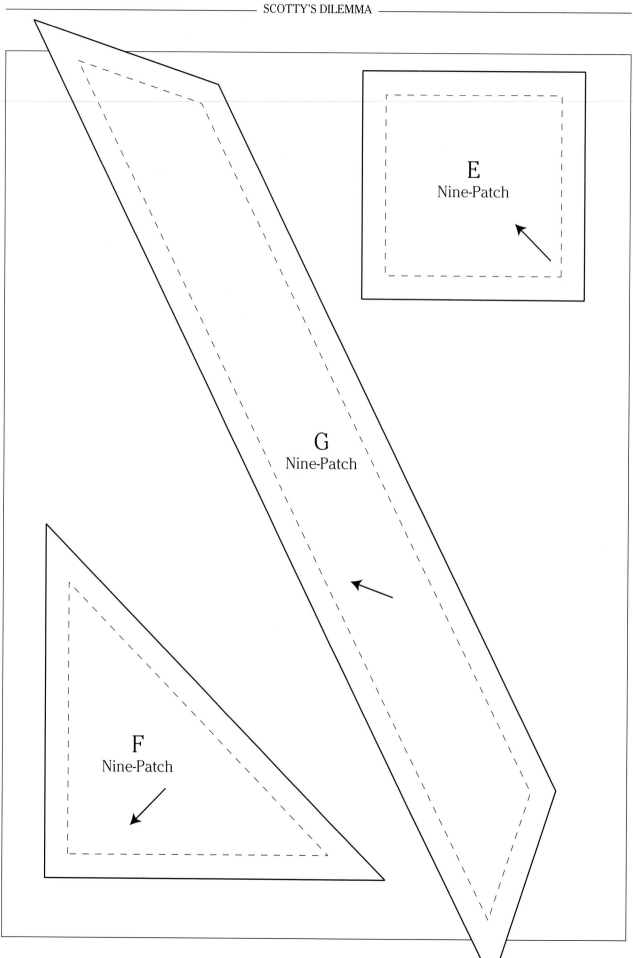

E
Nine-Patch

G
Nine-Patch

F
Nine-Patch

Chapter

4

What Others Have Done With Ties — Guest Quilters

BLEST BE THE TIES!

38" x 44", by Helen Kelley, ©1995,
machine pieced and hand quilted.

Helen Kelley, a witty columnist for *Quilter's Newsletter Magazine*, first made this quilt using the Dutch Mill pattern which she found in *The Collector's Dictionary of Quilt Names and Patterns* after a trip to Holland where she collected some local fabrics. Doesn't it translate beautifully using neck-ties? Helen sent along a page from a calendar with this quote about ties: "Diner's Dilemma – A clean tie attracts the soup of the day."

Techniques

Templates with seam allowance

Traditional piecing

Appliqué (optional)

FOR THE BLEST BE THE TIES QUILT

Section of Quilt	Fabric	# of Ties	Yardage	Template	# to Cut
	Neckties	12		A	1 each
				B	1 each
				C	1 each
				D	1 each
Background	Cotton		2 yards	E	12
				F	48
				G	48
				H	48
				I*	12
				J*	8
				K	4
Corners	Cotton		⅜ yard – 44" wide	22" squares cut into 2 triangles	2
Frame	Cotton			¼ yard strip	1¾" x 36"
Backing			1⅜ yard		
Binding			¼ yard		
Fabric for appliqué			¼ yard		

* Option: Cut templates I and J and according to the chart or cut half-square triangles for I (cut ten squares 6⅝"). Set aside eight

Helen's Notes

• Choose 12 different ties to make this quilt, even though it requires only nine 8" blocks. This allows you to discard any blocks that don't work because of fiber content or weave. It also allows you a choice of blocks that work best together.

• Choose ties made of wool, silk, rayon, and polyester. Use 100% cotton as a background fabric to stabilize all those slippery fabrics.

• After picking the ties apart, washing, and ironing them, hold them up to the light to discover any worn areas. These can be marked with small safety pins so you don't cut from those areas. Spray starch helps stabilize the fabrics. Set the iron setting between perma-press and cotton and approach each tie carefully to be sure it doesn't melt. At this point, stabilize the ties by pressing a fusible feather-weight or light-weight interfacing (PELLON®). (Helen didn't do this, but wishes she had.) If you don't use interfacing, read on for additional hints.

- If you have a variable speed on your machine, set it at half speed. You will not notice the slower speed as you work, but you will discover that you are much, much more accurate.

- Piece these blocks as you would piece any cotton block, being scrupulous in cutting and piecing, using *exactly* ¼" seams and making sure the edges come exactly even. When adding the four long triangles in each block, pin them carefully (lots of pins), matching the outer edges exactly. Then, sew from the outer edge to the inner point.

It is good to remember that as far as bias edges are concerned, it can be stretched out of shape but it can be eased into place. If you have cut precisely, pinned and sewn precisely, and eased in along the biases, the blocks will go together. They may get distorted, though PELLON® will prevent this. *Do not trim away or sew wider seams to compensate for any distortion.* Even though the blocks may be warped, if they are cut and pieced accurately, when they are sewn together, they will "heal" later when the entire piece is assembled.

- Of the 12 blocks Helen made for this quilt, one simply would not behave itself and it was deep-sixed. That left 11 blocks to choose from for the quilt. Choose the best pieced blocks for your quilt.

Sewing Instructions

- Sew pieces A, B, F, C, D, and G together as follows. Make four sets (Fig. 52).
- Sew the above sets to pieces H and E as follows (Fig. 53).

Note that the corner blocks are joined with three I pieces and one J, the center block has four J pieces and the other four blocks are joined with K (Fig. 54).

- Lay out the pieced blocks and background templates I, J, and K, according to the diagram in Fig. 55.

Again, it is important that seams meet at the edges and be cut exactly ¼". When adding the triangles, note that the cut edge joining the block is bias. Pin the two outer edges, mark the center of the block edge and the center of the triangle edge, and pin them together. If necessary, ease the bias edge of the triangle into place along the edge of the block with pins.

- Sew and press the block units.
- Stitch the block units together.
- The center medallion of the quilt measures 30" plus seam allowance.

Framing (Lattice)

- Stitch a 1¾" x 36" strip to the bias edge of a large corner triangle (half of a 22" square). The frame strip is longer than the triangle.
- Center the triangle unit along the edge of the medallion. This unit is much longer than the 30" center medallion (Fig. 56).
- Start sewing ¼" from the edge, ending ¼" from the edge.
- Miter these edges by folding the fabric in and hand stitching (Fig. 56).
- Trim away excess seam allowance.
- Press.

The quilt can be finished at this point, but Helen has designed it so you can make it any size you want.

Adjusting Size (optional)

This quilt can be trimmed to make whatever size you may need. (Fig. 57)

- With an Omnigrid ruler, trim the top and bottom edges to within ¾" of the frame.
- With the ruler, trim the sides of the quilt 1¾" inside the frame.
- Cut two strips 1¼" wide by the width of the fabric and stitch them across the top and bottom of the quilt to finish the edge.

Finishing

- Press the finished quilt top.
- Baste to the quilt top to the batting and backing.
- Add appliquéd belts or other embellishment. There is no pattern for this as Helen ad libbed. You could fill the large corner triangle spaces with your own appliquéd belt design or use labels and buttons.

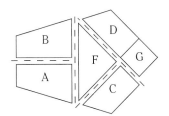

Fig. 52

Fig. 55

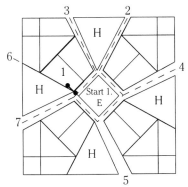

Fig. 53

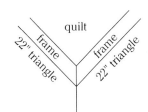

Fig. 56

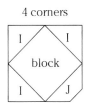

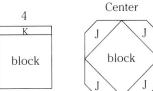

Fig. 54

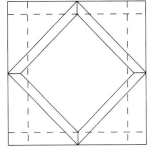

Trim along – – – –
if you wish

Fig. 57

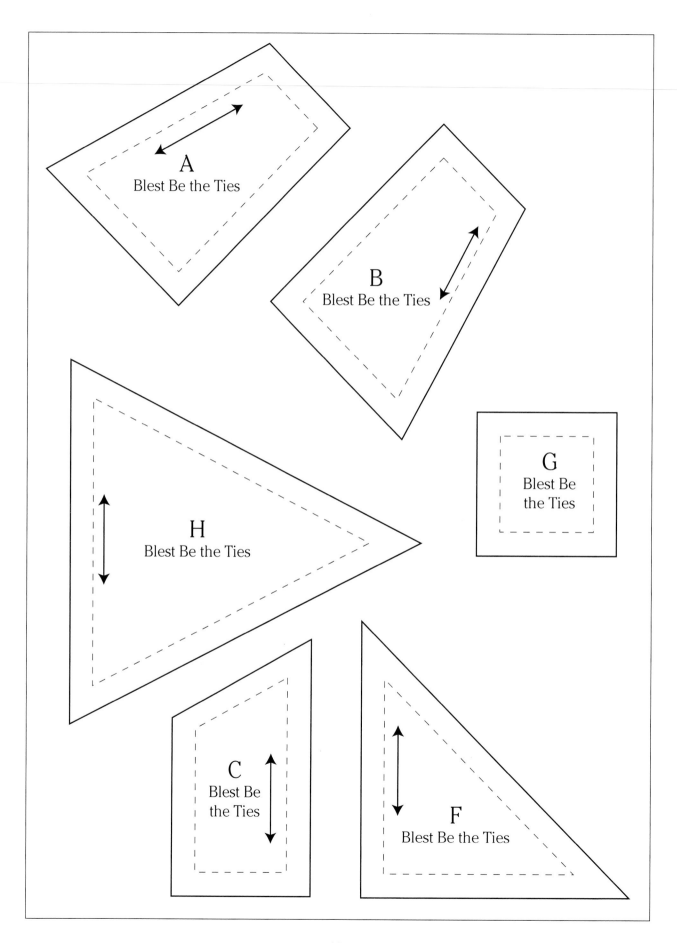

A
Blest Be the Ties

B
Blest Be the Ties

G
Blest Be
the Ties

H
Blest Be the Ties

C
Blest Be
the Ties

F
Blest Be the Ties

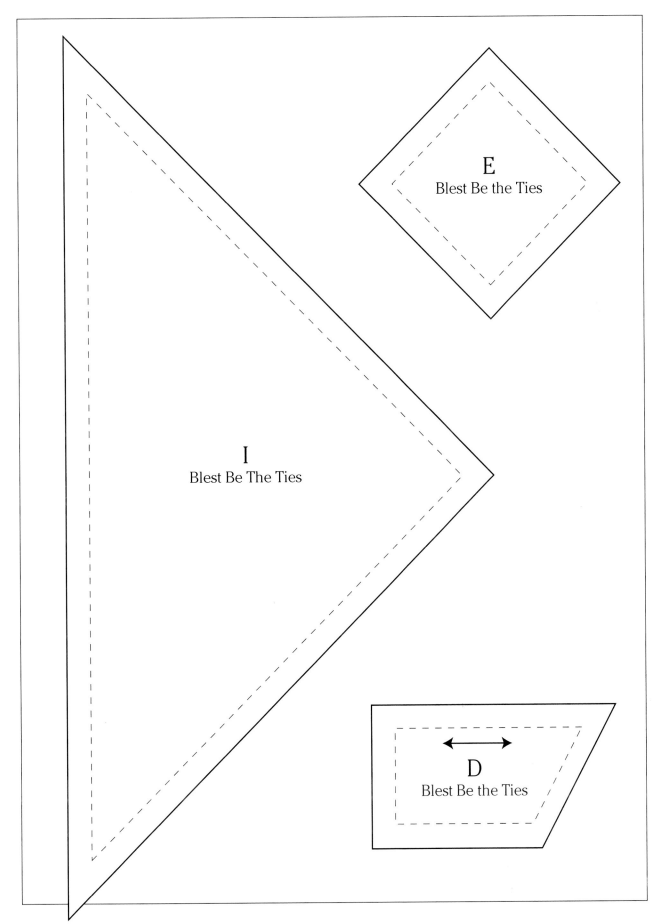

E
Blest Be the Ties

I
Blest Be The Ties

D
Blest Be the Ties

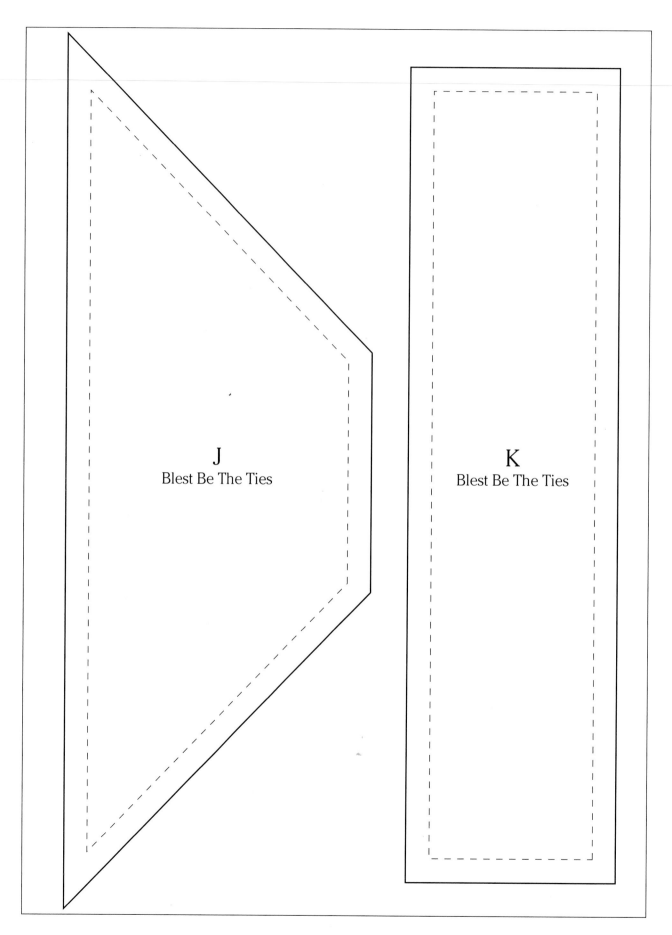

J
Blest Be The Ties

K
Blest Be The Ties

WINTER NIGHT NECKTIE LANDSCAPE

31½" x 33½", by Jo Diggs, ©1994.
hand appliquéd, then framed.

Jo is noted for her beautiful landscape quilts, clothing, wallhangings, and now matted appliqué pictures. Her pictures are well thought out, but done without patterns. Jo is experienced with hand appliqué so she didn't find it difficult working with neckties, finding only one or two raveling to the point of nastiness. She also used the reverse sides of some tie fabrics. Jo saved the wool open-weave stiffening from some of the ties. It will certainly show up in a manner we all wish we had thought of first.

Techniques
Appliqué on a muslin foundation

General Directions

- Assemble fabrics that please you and that you would like in a landscape.
- Use a range of fabrics, otherwise known as graded colors. It is better to have a wide range of small pieces than just a few large pieces.
- Start arranging the fabrics in possible use sequence. Ask yourself: If I use this for the sky, what will I use for hills? If I use these for hills, what will I have left for the ground?
- Plan the color sequence before cutting any shapes.
- The necktie you choose for the sky will probably determine the scale of the landscape, unless you are willing to piece the sky, in which case you can create a landscape of any size.
- Cut out simple shapes of hills, ground, and foreground, and arrange them on a muslin foundation. Shift the layering until you are satisfied with the layout. Jo never starts to sew until the whole piece is laid out completely.
- Stitch from the top down (you can baste the sky to the foundation layer); that is, the farthest most distant mountain is the first piece to get stitched down.
- After you stitch down the first hill, flip it back and trim any layers extending underneath (except for the foundation layer). Continue this stitching down and trimming underneath sequence throughout the whole landscape.

Jo's Notes:

When cutting the shapes, it is best to cut the edge that will show to the exact shape you want. Leave extra fabric on the bottom of the shape, the part that will be overlapped eventually, so that there is leeway for the fabric to shift as it is sewn and for possible changes you may want to make as the work progresses.

The nice thing about layering is that you can always put in another. There is a huge "fudge factor" in layered landscapes. More layers mean more colors and that is usually to the good.

Jo uses a whip stitch, shown below in Fig. 58.

She turns under the appliquéed edge ⅛", never ¼" which is too wide and makes the edge much harder to shape nicely.

Good ideas for layered landscapes come from greeting cards and advertisements which have already been somewhat abstracted or simplified, as opposed to a photograph which may tell more than you (especially a beginner) need to know.

Jo did not quilt her piece. The finished picture can be matted at a frame/art store.

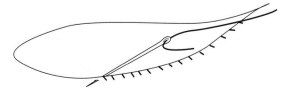

Fig. 58

1930'S SILK NECKTIE CRAZY QUILT

26" x 26", by Eila Tegethoff, 1994,
crazy patchwork.

Most of us are intrigued with crazy quilts because of the wonderful fabrics and stitches. Eila has made beautiful wallhangings and has such helpful, encouraging instructions, we will all be crazy quilting with our ties. She got me to try it (see my Bergdorf's Again holiday jacket, Chapter 7) and it was a lot of fun.

Tie fabrics look great in crazy quilts because of the variety of patterns and textures. Eila's quilt uses ties from the conservative to the very wild. The placement of all these interesting fabrics, plus the embroidery, give a totally new life to these old ties.

Techniques

Hand or machine piecing to a muslin foundation
Embroidery

FOR THE 1930'S SILK NECKTIE CRAZY QUILT

Fabric	# of Ties	Yardage	# to Cut
Neckties	30 or more		
Muslin		⅝ yard	18 – 7" squares
Backing – Navy		1 yard	31" x 31" square

Silk embroidery thread such as Soie Perle or cotton embroidery floss.

Prework Hints

- If the neckties are vintage, carefully inspect them for wear and damage.
- Divide the neckties into color groupings of your choosing: green, orange, blue, burgundy, silver, pink; etc.
- Use one color grouping in each block. Eila was able to make four blocks from each color grouping.
- This quilt has 16 blocks. You may want to piece extra blocks as you go in case one or two blocks just don't fit in. You can always use the extra squares for a smaller project later.
- Do not try to plan where the blocks will go before all 16 are pieced. A crazy quilt should have a surprise look to it.

Sewing Instructions for Crazy Patching

- In general, cut the muslin foundation fabric ½" larger all around than the desired size of the finished project. For this project the muslin is cut 7" square (finished block size is 6").
- Cut the first piece of tie fabric into a triangle shape and pin it to the upper left-hand corner of the foundation. This is the only piece that is cut before it is sewn in place.
- Then place a second patch right side up against the edge of the first patch to check color and size.
- Flip it over with right sides together, pin and sew in place. Flowerhead pins are great for this.
- Trim the second patch smaller if you would like, and trim any edges which extend beyond the muslin square.
- Iron on the muslin side of the block.
- Continue adding patches this way until the muslin foundation is completely covered.
- See Fig. 59 for a suggested order of patches. Keep in mind that crazy patchwork is spontaneous and there is no right or wrong shape to cut or order to piece.
- Iron the finished block on the muslin side and staystitch ½" from the outside edge.

Embellishments

- Embroider each block, starting and stopping at each staystitching line. Using some of the stitches on pages 75 –76 which Eila gleaned from here and there or try some of the stitches from Dorothy Bond's little book *Crazy Quilt Stitches.*

    You might want to add an embroidered web and spider. Crazy quilting was at the height of its popularity in the Victorian era and Victorian ladies believed that embroidering a web and spider on a crazy quilt would bring good luck. Eila and I too find it a wonderful design feature. There seems to be no place a web won't fit – unless you happen to really dislike them. In that case, do not include one.

    Eila put a spider web in the center squares. She designed the web to fit the space, traced the shape onto typing paper, positioned it on the quilt, and embroidered around it.

    Eila used gold thread inside the squares and ecru thread to outline the squares and embroider the spider web. If your neckties are not too busy, you can achieve a real nice look by adding more color with your thread. Choose one shade lighter or one shade darker than the neckties used so that the stitching shows up well.

- After all embellishments are added to each patch, trim each block to 6¼" square.

Assembling

- Lay out your 16 or more pieced and embroidered blocks to decide how to assemble them. Turn the squares in any direction.

    Try to balance the colors. In this quilt the red blocks and the green/orange ones were problematic. Eila's solution was to put the red blocks in the center and, since the green orange ones really did not coordinate well with the rest of the piece, she put them on the outside corners. By rearranging the blocks, you can come up with many variations. Learn to trust your sense of color and balance. Ultimately the person you want to please is yourself.

- When you find a pleasing arrangement, mark the back of the muslin squares in the upper

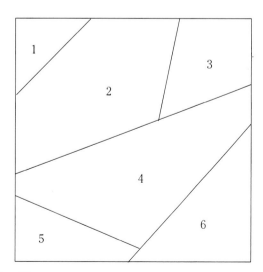

Fig. 59

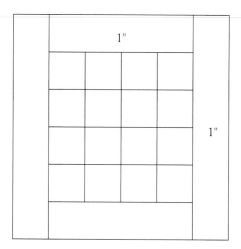

Fig. 60

left hand corner. Pencil in a dot, check, or number so that you don't lose your order and have to start all over again.

- Let the arrangement sit on a table for a few days so you can contemplate it.
- After you've made your final decision, sew the blocks together, one row at a time.

Finishing

- To finish the embellishments embroider (chain or feather stitch) on the seamlines to outline each square. Interesting labels from the neckties or elsewhere can be appliquéd or fancy stitched to the quilt top. Add tie tacks (which fasten neckties to shirts) and/or buttons at this time.
- To finish the quilt pin baste the quilt top to the backing. Batting is not necessary.
- Evenly fold the edges of the backing to the front, turn under the edge, and hand stitch in place. Miter the corners or sew them down as in Fig. 60.

1930's Silk Necktie Crazy Quilt Embellishments

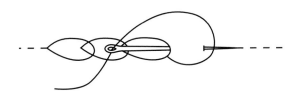

Chain Stitch

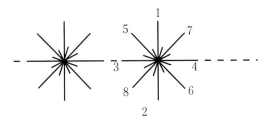

Star Stitch

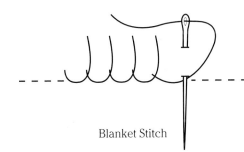

Blanket Stitch

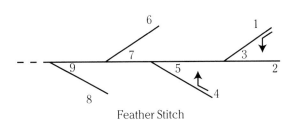

Feather Stitch

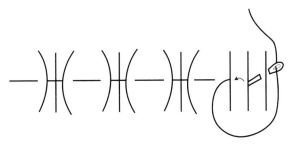

Haystack Stitch

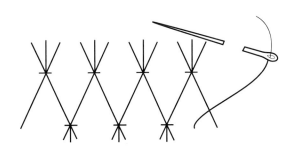

Herringbone Stitch

Spider Web – Couching Stitch

Spider – Chain Stitch legs
     – 3 strand floss
– beads or buttons for the body

Draw a large star and
then couch at even intervals.

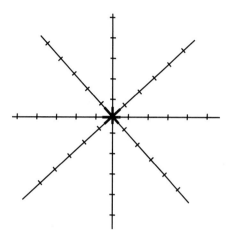

½ web

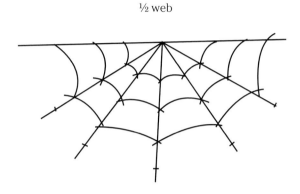

¼ web

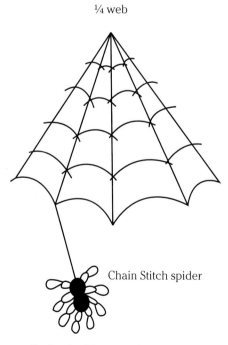

Full web with spider

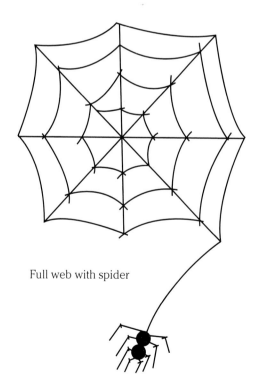

Chain Stitch spider

Body of spider – can be
french knots, buttons, or beads.

TIES IN THE SKY

30" x 30", by Dixie Haywood, 1995,
machine pieced and hand quilted.

Dixie had just culled her husband's ties and had given them to the Waterfront Mission. So she put an ad in her local quilt guild newsletter, explaining she needed a variety of ties for use in patchwork and quilting. Her plea for any ties that could be "given" away without causing a domestic disturbance yielded 150 to 175 ties! One bag came from a DEA agent, collected from police and drug enforcement agents in New York City, with a com-

ment that the agent knows why they wear dress suits – to cover these ties!

This quilt is simple to piece. It has so much movement, it looks like it's ready to spin off the page.

Techniques

Paper foundation piecing on freezer paper ("under pressed-piecing")
Needle-punching

TIES IN THE SKY

FOR THE TIES IN THE SKY QUILT

Fabric	# of Ties	Yardage
Light ties	2	
Gray ties	4	
Black ties	9	
Red ties	9	
Backing (muslin)		1 yard
Binding (pinstripe necktie)	1	
Freezer paper		

Under Pressed-Piecing with Freezer Paper Foundations

- Trace the pattern onto freezer paper. The easiest way to duplicate the pattern is to pin the traced pattern to layers of freezer paper and needle-punch (see Chapter 2 for instructions on needle-punching). Make 12 copies at a time. Be sure the same side of the freezer paper is facing up. The dull side up will give the mirror image result like the quilt shown here. The shiny side up will duplicate the pattern as printed. Trim the freezer paper to the finished block size.

    Option: Use muslin for the foundation squares, rather than freezer paper. The sewing instructions are the same, except that the muslin foundation is not removed.

- Make "rough-cut" templates as follows: Trace the pattern onto a piece of paper. Mark the grain lines on all pieces, number them like the pattern and cut them out. Lay the paper on the wrong side of the fabric and cut ½" on all sides for the templates. Dixie uses this wide seam allowance to prevent the seam from raveling and pulling out when the freezer paper is removed.

- These directions are for the mirror image version of the pattern. Using the paper templates, cut out all the pieces. In order for the star to "shine," arrange the colors so that piece #1 and piece #8 are the lightest and pieces #2, #3, and #9 are the darkest. The dark star is easily seen; squint your eyes to see the light star.

- Press baste piece #1 by lightly touching the tip of the iron in two or three spots, right side up, onto the shiny side of the freezer paper. Position the piece with an equal seam allowance on all sides of the needle-punched lines which are the stitching lines.

- Lay piece #2 in place, and follow the instructions for foundation piecing in Chapter 2,

page 26, until the block is complete.

- Stitch 36 blocks.

- Arrange the blocks according to the diagram below and stitch together the four-block sections (Fig. 61).

- Arrange and sew together the nine four-block sections – three across by three down.

Finishing

- Press the finished quilt top.

- Remove the freezer paper.

- Baste the finished quilt top to the backing and batting.

- Quilt. Dixie quilted concentric quarter-circles in each block. This simple quilting design adds even more movement to the quilt.

- Bind with a striped tie.

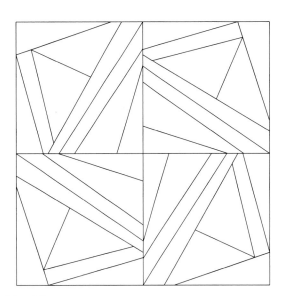

Fig. 61

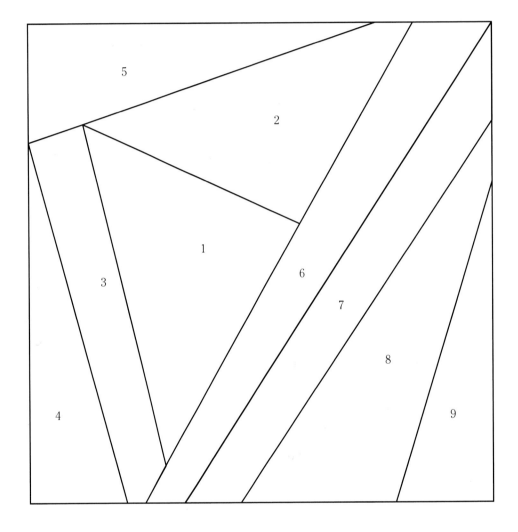

SILKY SCRAP PINEAPPLE

26" x 26", by Jane Hall ©1995,
machine pieced and hand quilted.

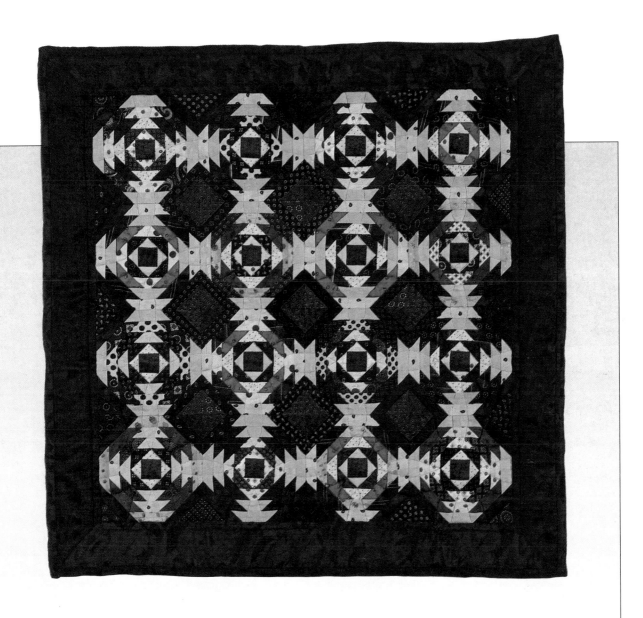

Jane was a natural to make a Pineapple quilt using ties since she is a master of foundation piecing. She is co-author of a book with Dixie Haywood called *Firm Foundations*. Working with ties was a first for her.

This quilt makes great use of ties which are on the conservative side. It's an elegant quilt, with an antique look and strong graphic design.

Silky Scrap Pineapple has 16 blocks. Jane used some ties, a bag of silk scraps from a tie factory, and a few strips of silk or polyester from yardage and a scarf. The border is patterned silk (yardage).

Techniques

Paper foundation piecing
Needle-punching

SILKY SCRAP PINEAPPLE

FOR THE SILKY SCRAP PINEAPPLE QUILT

Piece	Fabric	# of Ties	Yardage	# to Cut
Diagonal	Dark ties*	4		50" cut into 1½" strips
Horizontal/Vertical	Light ties*	4		45" cut into 1½" strips
Corners	Dark tie	1		10" cut into 2½" strips or 2 – 2½" strips cut on the diagonal into 4 triangles
Center Squares	Red tie	1		16 – 2" squares
Border			½ yard	4– 3½" x 26½" strips
* Tie fabrics can be repeated in the blocks. Jane used reds, whites, and blues.				
Hint: Place the fabric strips on the perforated side of the paper which helps hold them down as they are sewn.				

The pineapple pattern depends on sharp value contrast for its graphics. Light colors were used for all the horizontal and vertical strips and dark strips for all the diagonal strips. Dark blues for diagonal strip #4 create outlines around the corner squares. The colors and patterning of the centers and the corners were also controlled so that the design was consistent and had good contrast – all the centers are red, the corners around the outside edge are all dark, and the corners within the quilt are red.

For this project Jane decided to leave the papers in for stability which works well on wall-hangings. If you make a bed-size quilt, consider using fabric foundations.

Sewing Sequence

- Pin a center square (red) onto the rough side of the foundation, making sure the fabric covers the center square with adequate seam allowance on all sides.
- Note: all the strips for the logs are cut 1½" wide. Cut four pieces of the first light fabric (#1), each the length of the center square (1") plus 1" (½" seam allowance on all sides) = 2".
- Place the first light piece along one side of the center square of fabric, right sides together, matching the cut edges.
- Pin the strip, placing the pin toward the bottom of the strip, away from the seamline.
- Turn the foundation over so that the side with the tie fabric is against the feed dogs.
- Stitch on the line, beginning and ending two to three stitches before and after the line. Use a smaller than usual stitch length.
- Trim threads and any excess seam allowance.
- Flip open the strip and press. Pin in place.
- Repeat, sewing another light strip (#1) onto the opposite side of the center square. Then stitch light strips onto the two remaining sides.

- Row 2 will use the first dark fabric, #2. Cut four pieces the size of the sewing line for #2 (1½" plus 1") 2½".
- Stitch each in place, sewing opposite sides as before. It is possible to pin two opposite strips in place and stitch them consecutively, hopping from the end of the first seam to the beginning of the second. Working with the slippery bias strips, Jane found it necessary to use two or more pins with each strip to hold them perfectly straight. It is important not to stretch the strips as you lay them in place.
- Continue to piece rows of four light strips (#1, #3, #5, #7) and then four dark strips (#2, #4, #6, #8). To determine the length of each strip, measure the length of each row on the pattern and add seam allowance, ½" each side.
- The outside corner rows are wider than the other strips (2½"). Stitch in place.
- Press all blocks.
- Join all blocks together in rows.

Border

- Mark in 3½" on each end of the border strips.
- Pin to the quilt ¼" in from the edge of the quilt.
- Stitch all border strips in place from pin to pin.
- Miter the corners as in TAILSPIN – TIESPIN, Chapter 3, page 38.

Finishing

- Press the finished quilt top.
- Baste the quilt top to the batting and backing.
- Quilt ¼" around all pieces.
- Bind the edges with the backing fabric.

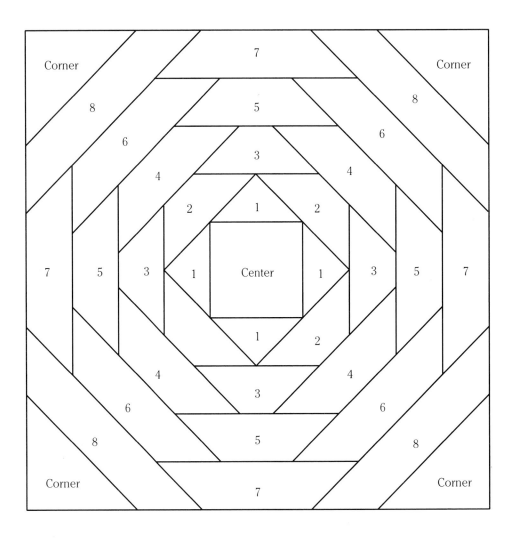

Chapter

5

More Great Patterns

The quilts in this chapter are a little more difficult than those in Chapter 3,
but with a little perseverance, I know you can do it!

HAPPY BIRTHDAY ALLAN

34" x 38", by Janet B. Elwin, ©1992,
machine pieced and machine quilted, in the Beres collection, Falls Church, VA.

When I was a child, the quilt on my bed was a soft yellow Dresden Plate which I always thought looked like neckties. It was only natural that I first used neckties in a Dresden Plate variation.

This quilt, Happy Birthday, Allan, is also a great way to celebrate the retirement of your favorite wearer of business clothes (and to make good use of his ties and shirts). It is even embellished with those little white shirt buttons.

Sewing Sequence
Assembling Plates

- Cut out the plate segments (piece A) from the 12 different neckties.
- Fold the tie fabric for each plate segment in half, right sides together, stitch across the wide end and trim the point (Fig. 62).

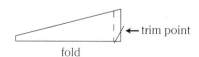

← trim point

fold

Fig. 62

Techniques

Templates
Traditional Piecing
Appliqué
Button Embellishment

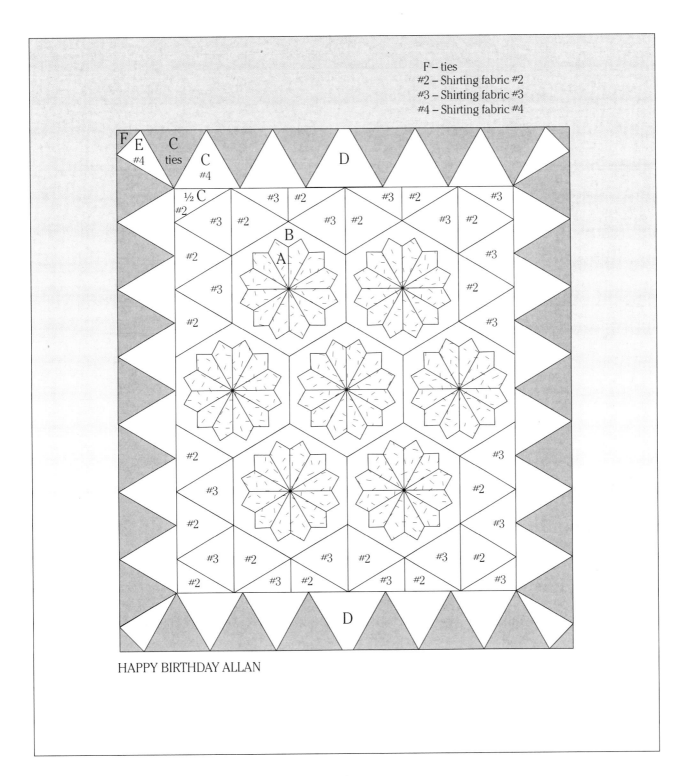

F – ties
#2 – Shirting fabric #2
#3 – Shirting fabric #3
#4 – Shirting fabric #4

HAPPY BIRTHDAY ALLAN

FOR THE HAPPY BIRTHDAY ALLAN QUILT

Fabric	# of Ties	Yardage	Template	# to Cut
Neckties	12		A*	7 each
			C	2 each from 10
				3 each from 2
			F	4
Shirting #1		1 yard	B*	7
Shirting #2		½ yard	C	12
			half C	3
			half CR	3
Shirting #3		½ yard	C	12
			half C	3
			half CR	3
Shirting #4		½ yard	C	20
			D	2
			E	4
Backing		1 yard		
Binding – ties	1 or 2			

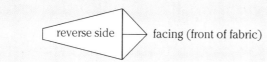

Fig. 63

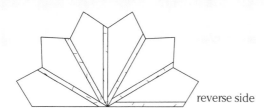

Fig. 64

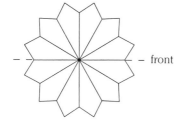

Fig. 65

- Turn inside out, line the seam up at the center and press, forming a facing (Fig. 63).
- With right sides together, stitch the ties together two at a time (six sets). Fingerpress the seams to the left. Arrange three sets in a semi-circle. Stitch together the center pair to the left pair. Fingerpress the seam to the left. Stitch together the completed section to the right pair. Fingerpress the seam to the right (Fig. 64).
- Repeat Step 7 for the lower half of the plate. Pin the two halves together and stitch across (Fig. 65).

Preparing Background

- The background is formed of large hexagons. To create guidelines for placing the completed Dresden Plates onto the background, iron the hexagons in half, and then in thirds, lining up the edges (Fig. 66).

- Arrange the necktie plates so that the seams line up along the creases. Pin in place. Either hand appliqué, top stitch or buttonhole stitch by hand or machine (Pfaff stitch #12) along the edges of the plates (Fig. 67).

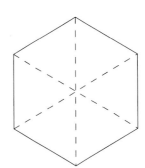

Fig. 66

Piecing the Quilt

Hexagons

Piece the hexagons (piece B) together. Stitch, starting in ¼" and ending ¼" from the edge of the fabric (Fig. 68).

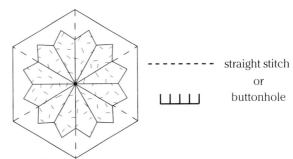

- - - - - - - - - straight stitch
or
⊔⊔⊔⊔ buttonhole

Triangle Background

- Shirting fabrics #2 and #3 form the background. Stitch triangles from fabric #2 and triangles from fabric #3 together to create six diamonds. Set in as a diamond, working from the center out, starting ¼" in from the edge of the fabric, stitching to the edge of the fabric (Fig. 68).
- Use shirting fabrics #2 and #3 to make the corner sets (large triangles). Follow the numbered sequence in the diagram (Fig. 69). Stitch the corner sets in place.

Fig. 67

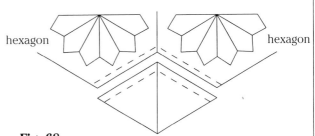

hexagon   hexagon

Fig. 68

Borders

- Stitch together two strips of triangles (C & D) to form the top and bottom borders. Note: Template I is in the center of the row (Fig. 70).
- Stitch the strips to the top and bottom of the quilt, leaving ¼" free at the ends of each seam.
- Stitch the four corner sets (E and F) (Fig. 71).
- Stitch together two strips of triangles (C) for the side borders, and add the corner sets (Fig. 72, page 90).
- Stitch the side borders to the quilt, leaving ¼" free at the ends of each seam. Sew the seams at the corners, stitching from the center to the outside, starting ¼" in and

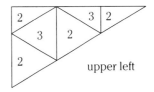

Fig. 69

upper left

Fig. 70

Fig. 71

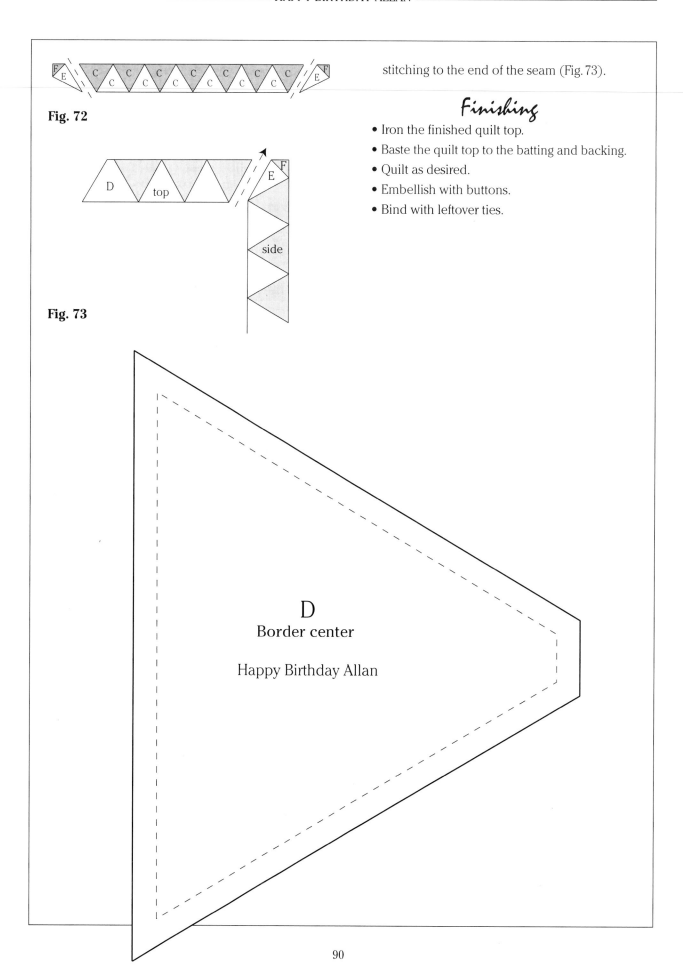

Fig. 72

Fig. 73

stitching to the end of the seam (Fig. 73).

Finishing

- Iron the finished quilt top.
- Baste the quilt top to the batting and backing.
- Quilt as desired.
- Embellish with buttons.
- Bind with leftover ties.

D
Border center

Happy Birthday Allan

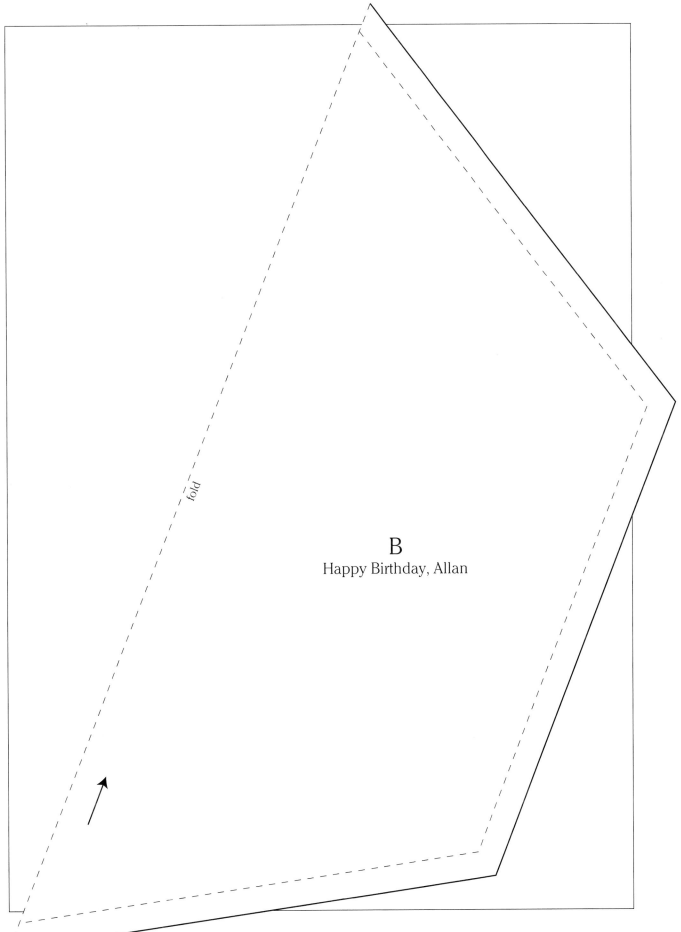

fold

B
Happy Birthday, Allan

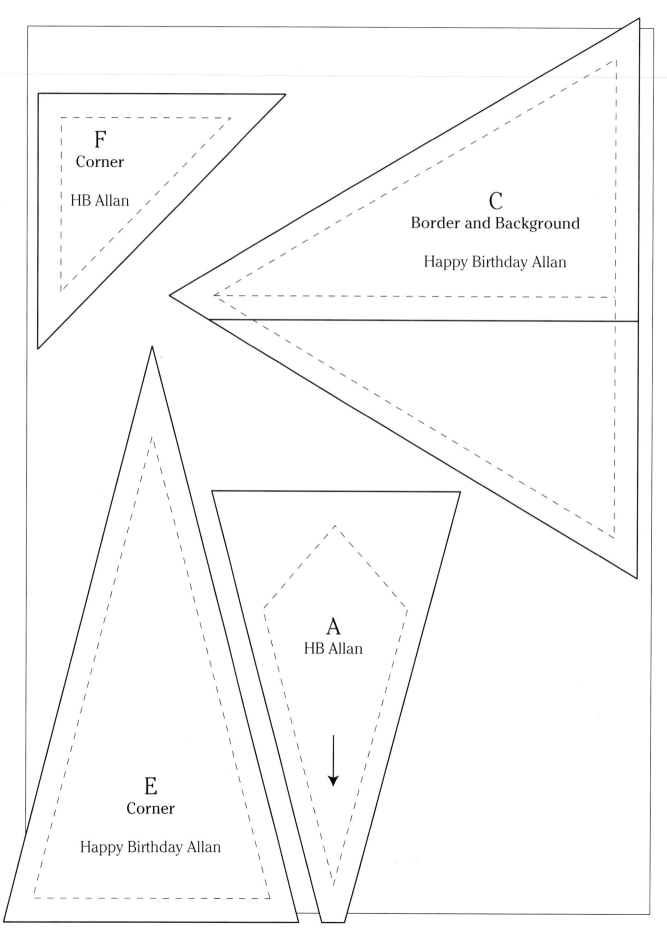

F
Corner

HB Allan

C
Border and Background

Happy Birthday Allan

E
Corner

Happy Birthday Allan

A
HB Allan

SUNRISE AND EVENING STAR

48" x 68", by Janet B. Elwin, ©1993,
machine pieced and machine quilted, in the Elwin collection.

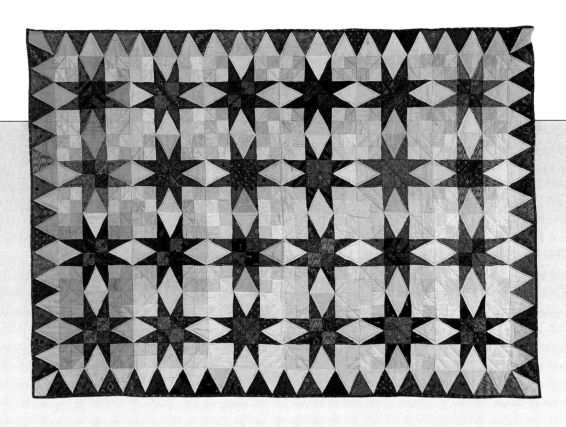

Sunrise and evening star,
And one clear call for me!
And may there be no moaning of the bar,
When I put out to sea.

from *Crossing the Bar*
by Alfred Tennyson (1809–92)

You will like some designs better than others and with those you feel are real winners, make a full-size quilt. Making just one block of a pattern is an experiment. Some may work better with your choice of ties and background fabrics than others. If you don't like the results, reread Chapter 2 carefully. Because the weights of your tie fabrics may vary from what I used, you might revise or use different techniques. Please feel free to make any necessary adjustments and whether to cut fabrics on-grain or off-grain. I call this a tester block. If I am satisfied, I proceed to cut out the rest of the quilt and work away.

This quilt uses the Fifty-Four, Forty or Fight block made with brand new necktie fabric samples given to me during my trip to Japan in 1992. Over 80 rayon drapery samples were used for the background fabric. This bunch was given to me by a California quilt guild trying to unload them – a very happy combination.

Techniques

Templates
Traditional Piecing
Drapery samples (optional)
Flannel board layout (optional)

SUNRISE AND EVENING STAR

For the Sunrise and Evening Star Quilt

Fabric	# of Ties	Yardage	Template	# to Cut
Blue to dark grey ties	24		A	4 each
			B	4 each
			BR	4 each
Background for blocks		2¼ yards*	C	96
			A	384
Border triangles – use the above ties			C	3 each (with a few extra)
Border background*		⅝ yard	C	60
			D	4
Backing		2½ yards		
Binding – leftover ties				

* Background fabric yardage is for a single fabric. If you're using multiple fabrics for the background, figure at least ¾ yard for every two blocks.

Fabric Preparation

- Each block uses three different tie fabrics. Sort as follows: divide the ties into 24 piles with one tie fabric (1) for each block. Then mix and match to add two coordinating tie fabrics (2 and 3) to each block. The diagram right shows the placement of the three fabrics (Fig. 74).

- If using multiple background fabrics, lay out the pieces on a flannel board. For small pieces of rayon drapery samples, cut as much as you can from each piece, keeping in mind it is better to work with lots of pieces so you have more to choose from. I used off-white, beige, palest of pinks to rosy pinks, and a few salmon.

Stitching Sequence

- Follow the diagram Fig. 75 to piece 24 star blocks.

- Stitch the blocks together in rows, six across by four down.

Border

- Make two strips for the side borders using triangle (C): 12 light and 13 dark. Make two strips for the top and bottom borders using 18 light C, 19 dark C, and 2 light D (corner piece).

- Lay out the triangles according to the diagram, with the dark ones on the outside edges. Stitch the alternating dark and light triangles together, with the dark triangles on the ends. SUNRISE AND EVENING STAR diagram, page 94.

- Sew one piece D to each end of the top and bottom borders.

- Stitch the side borders to the quilt first.

- Then stitch on the top and bottom borders.

- Sew the corner seams, stitching D to the adjacent C.

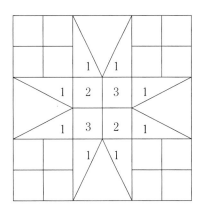

Fig. 74

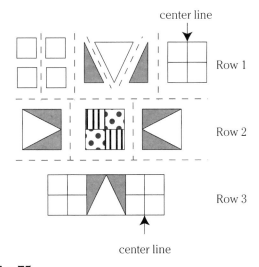

Fig. 75

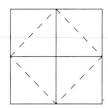

Fig. 76

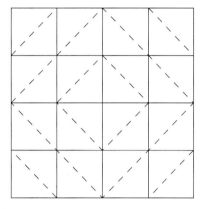

Fig. 77

Finishing

- Press the finished quilt top.
- Baste to the quilt top to the batting and backing.
- Quilt ¼" away from the seams on pieces B and C. Quilt diagonal lines as in the diagrams left Figs. 76 and 77.
- Bind with leftover ties.

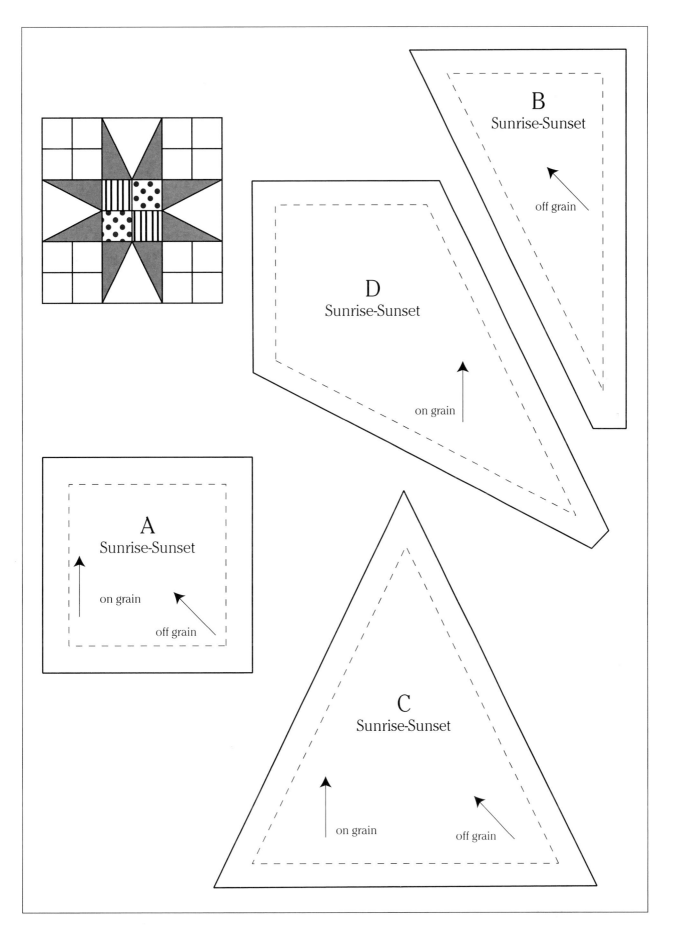

B
Sunrise-Sunset

off grain

D
Sunrise-Sunset

on grain

A
Sunrise-Sunset

on grain

off grain

C
Sunrise-Sunset

on grain

off grain

MY HEART BELONGS TO DADDY

38¼" x 41¾", by Janet B. Elwin, ©1995,
machine pieced and machine quilted, in the Elwin collection.

I accidentally stumbled onto this design when I made a pieced back for my Hot Flashes quilt (*Creative Triangles for Quilters*, Chilton, 1995.) Neckties and daddy's girl just seemed to fit and I couldn't resist taking the heart motif from the reverse side of Hot Flashes and turning it into a repetitive pattern.

This would make a great quilt for your spouse, sweetheart, or other beloved person in your life, perhaps for an anniversary or Valentine's Day present.

Techniques

Traditional Piecing

Template without seam allowance

Set-in seams or pivot method

Rayon background fabrics with flannel board layout (optional)

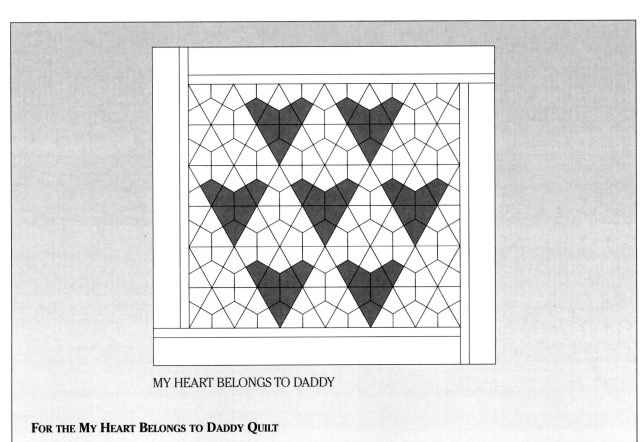

MY HEART BELONGS TO DADDY

FOR THE MY HEART BELONGS TO DADDY QUILT

Section of Quilt	Fabric	# of Ties	Yardage	Template	# to Cut
Background	Rayon drapery samples or			A	189
	3 similar solids or prints		¾ yard each	A	63 each
Hearts	Red ties	7		A	7 each
Highlighter	Pink /red tie	1			2 strips ⅞" x 35⅞"*
					2 strips ⅞" x 39⅜"*
Border	Red tie	4			2 strips 3" x 35⅞"*
					2 strips 3" x 39⅜"*
Binding	Ties	2			
Backing			1 yard		

* Measurement includes seam allowance.

Preparation

This quilt is made from a single template, arranged in a triangle formation. The placement of the red tie pieces forms the hearts. There is no template for cutting half pieces for the edges of the background, as I think it is much easier to use the whole piece of fabric, stitch, and then trim the edges.

If you are using a huge variety of shades for the background, lay out all the background pieces and the ties on a flannel board until you have a pleasing color arrangement. You may want to cut out extra pieces to give you more to chose from. If using three closely related solids or prints for the background, arrange the pieces in triangles sets (see diagram on page 99).

Sewing

Piecing can be done by the set-in method or the pivot method as follows.

Set-In Piecing Method

- Use Template A which has no seam allowance. Mark your fabrics and cut ¼" seam allowance by eye.
- On Pieces 1, 2, and 3, insert a pin ¼" from the corner as shown in Fig. 78. This marks the center of the triangle unit.

- Match the pins and stitch Piece 2 to Piece 3, stitching from the pins to the edge of the fabric. The ¼" unsewn seam allowance is necessary to set in Piece 1.
- Pin Piece 1 to Piece 3. Stitch on the seamline from the center, ¼" from the edge, out to the edge of the fabric.
- Pin Piece 1 to Piece 2 and stitch as above.
- Press the seams.
- Lay the pieced triangle unit in its spot on the flannel board.
- Continue piecing all the triangles in the same manner.

Pivot Method

- Stitch Pieces 2 and 3 together according to the above instructions for set-in piecing.
- Finger press the seam to the right (looking at the front side of the fabrics).
- Pin Piece 1 to Piece 2. Stitch from the edge of the fabric to the seamline in the center of the triangle unit. Then, with the sewing machine needle down, lift the presser foot and pull Piece 1 around to line it up with Piece 3. Stitch over the seam allowance to the edge of the fabric (Fig. 79).
- Continue with the last 3 steps for the set-in piecing method.

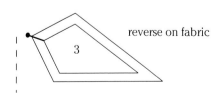
reverse on fabric

Fig. 78

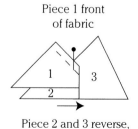
Piece 1 front of fabric

Piece 2 and 3 reverse, seam to right.

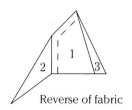
Reverse of fabric

Fig. 79

Edge Pieces

- For the edge pieces on the left side of the quilt, stitch Piece 1 to Piece 3, stitching from the edge of the cloth to the edge of the cloth along the marked line.
- For the edge pieces on the right side of the quilt, stitch Piece 1 to Piece 2 as above.

Quilt Assembly

- Stitch the rows of triangle units together, finger pressing the seams in Row 1 to the right, Row 2 to the left, and so on, alternating for each row. Pin the seam on the front side in the direction it is pressed to easily keep track of which row is going in what direction (Figs. 80 and 81).
- Stitch the rows together. The alternating directions of the pressed seams will make the quilt go together more smoothly.
- Press the finished quilt top.
- With a ruler and rotary cutter, trim the edges of the quilt straight, adding ¼" seam allowance (Fig. 82).

Highlighter and Border

- Stitch the highlighter strips to the border pieces.
- Sew the border to the quilt top in the Log Cabin style. Start by marking in 6" on the left side of the first border.
- Mark 3" in on the quilt and pin from the mark, easing in the fabric if necessary.
- Stitch the second border strip, covering the end of the first strip and sewing to the edge of the quilt. Repeat for the remaining border strips.
- Remove the pin from first border. Finish sewing the seam for the first border to the edge of the quilt, covering the end of the fourth border.

Finishing

- Baste the quilt top to the batting and backing.
- Quilt ¼" inside the hearts. Then echo quilt ¼" from the first line of quilting, repeating the heart motif. Echo quilt in as far as you can. Quilt straight lines ¼" apart in the background. Quilt in-the-ditch on the highlighter strip. Using a paper ruler, quilt at 1¼" intervals on the diagonal. Machine stitch hearts (Pfaff program #164).

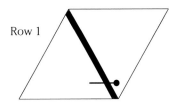

Fig. 80

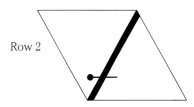

Fig. 81

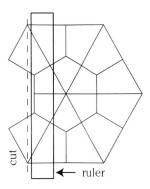

Fig. 82

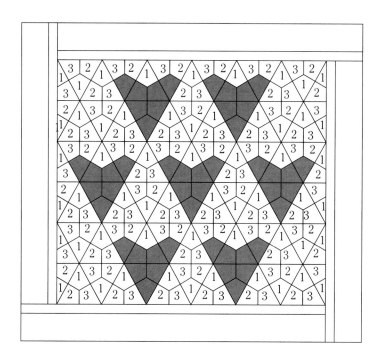

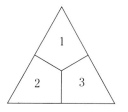

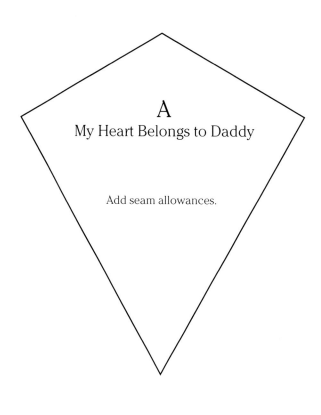

A
My Heart Belongs to Daddy

Add seam allowances.

Chapter

6

Are You Ready For a Quilt?

FOR A LONG TALL SLEEPER

58" x 98", by Mildred Patterson, 1988–89,
hand pieced, in the Patterson collection.

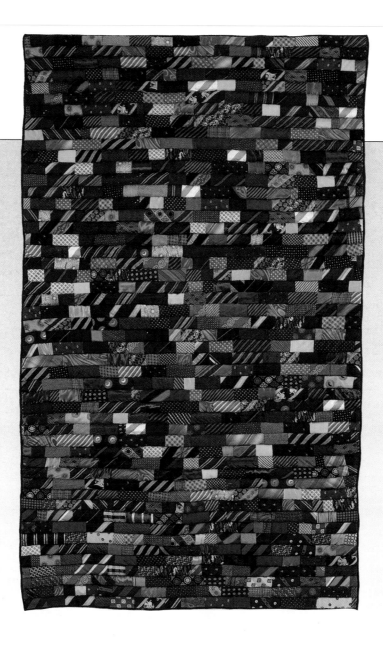

Mildred saw a quilt in *Lady's Circle Patchwork Quilts*, Fall 1983, called A Time Gone By, which inspired this rendition. Her ties were given to her from a friend.

This quilt is constructed in an unusual way –

tubes of strip-pieced fabric are stuffed with batting and sewn to a fabric foundation. The result is a three-dimensional quilt which is interesting artistically and really warm to sleep under.

Techniques

Foundation piecing in five sections
No templates
Strip-piecing
Tying the quilt

FOR THE FOR A LONG TALL SLEEPER QUILT

Fabric	# of Ties	Yardage	# to Cut
Neckties	Approx. 90		3"wide x 2" to 7"long, strips
Bright colored satin and polyester		70 pieces – ⅛ yard each	3"wide x 2" to 4"long, strips
Muslin		3½ yards	5 pieces 22" x 61"
Backing: Patterned polyester		4⅛ yards	
Binding: Black satin		⅝ yard	
Batting		1 package	
Black crochet thread			

Preparation

- Mark parallel pencil lines on both sides of a muslin piece. Make the lines 61" long, 2" apart, leaving a 1" margin at the top and bottom. Mark "top" and "bottom" on each piece.
- Arrange the tie fabric pieces into long strips in a pleasing color arrangement.
  HINT: Using the reverse side of the pieces helps to vary the colors. Add several non-tie fabrics in each row for variety.
- Sew by hand or machine the arranged pieces into 61" strips, each 3" wide.
- Arrange the completed 61" strips so that most vertical seams will not meet when the strips are joined.
- Prepare the batting by cutting strips 2" x 61". For extra loft, double strips of batting were used.

Sewing

- Lay the first tie strip right side up on a muslin foundation, with the top edge ½" above the top drawn line.
- Pin the strip to the foundation.
- Turn the foundation over and stitch exactly on the top drawn line on the back of the foundation, through the muslin and the strip.
- Working from the front, fold the tie strip back over the sewing line and place a batting strip between the first two drawn lines on the foundation.
- Pull the tie strip down to cover the batting and pin it to the second drawn line, leaving a ½" seam allowance. Baste along this seamline to anchor the strip and the enclosed batting.
- Place the second tie strip right side down on

top of the first strip, matching the basted line of the first strip with an edge of the second strip. Pin.

- Turn the foundation over and stitch along the second line, through all the layers.
- From the front, fold the second tie strip back over the sewing line and place a double batting strip between the seamline just stitched and the next drawn line.
- Pull the tie strip down to cover the batting and pin it to the third drawn line, allowing a ½" seam allowance. Baste in place, add the next tie strip, pin, turn the foundation over, and stitch along the line as before.
- Repeat the first nine steps to complete the ten rows of the first section.
- Sew the remaining four sections the same way as the first section.

Assembling

- Place the first two sections together, right sides facing together. Pin the top of the second section to the bottom of the first section, matching the drawn lines.
- Sewing on the foundation side, stitch exactly on the drawn lines.
- Join the other sections, matching the bottom line of one to the top line of the next.

Finishing

- Trim the edges on all sides.
- Baste the finished quilt top to the backing.
- Bind with black satin.
- From the back, with black crochet thread, tie the backing to the top, spacing the knots 8" apart in every fourth seam. This will not show from the front.

AUCTION PIECES

93½" x 93½", by Susannah Vogel, 1994,
machine pieced and hand quilted, in the Vogel collection.

The tie fabrics in this quilt have a long history. Susannah's 180 tie fabric scraps of 75 different patterns were bought at an auction 25 years before the quilt was made. A friend of Susannah's was given them by an aunt. Then Susannah received them and passed them on to her daughter. Her daughter thought there wasn't enough of a single fabric pattern to form a design so they bounced back to Susannah who just started making blocks, randomly selecting colors as she went.

Techniques

Templates including seam allowance
Traditional piecing

FOR THE AUCTION PIECES QUILT

Fabric	# of Ties	Yardage	Template	# to Cut
Neckties	242		Triangle #1	484 (2 each)
Backing: cotton		6½ yards		

* This quilt can be made with fewer ties in a smaller size.

Janet's Hint: Susannah cautioned about the difficulty of sewing bias edges and fraying fabrics. If this is a concern, use PELLON® to stabilize them.

Sewing Sequence

Four triangles make up each block. Make 121 blocks for this queen size quilt – 11 blocks across by 11 blocks down.

- Sew four triangles to make one block as in the diagram (Fig. 83).

- Make 121 blocks. Press all blocks.
- Arrange the blocks in a pleasing color placement.
- Sew into rows. You will be sewing bias edge to bias edge. Be careful not to stretch it too much. Each finished row should measure 93½".
- Sew the rows together, pinning seams carefully.

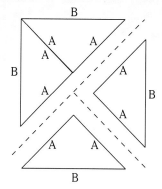

Fig. 83

Finishing

- Press the finished quilt top.
- Baste the quilt top, batting, and backing together, leaving 2½" of backing beyond the edge of the quilt top all around.
- Quilt as desired. Susannah quilted to de-emphasize the individual blocks by quilting diagonally through four-block sets (Fig. 84).
- Trim backing to extend 2" around the edges of the quilt top.
- Trim the batting to extend ¾" around edges of the top.
- To bind the quilt, fold the backing to the front and turn the edges under. Fold carefully to form an even ¾" finished edge. Pin and hand sew in place.

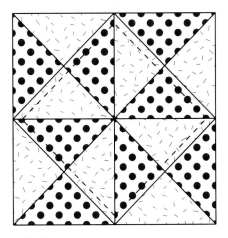

4 blocks

Fig. 84

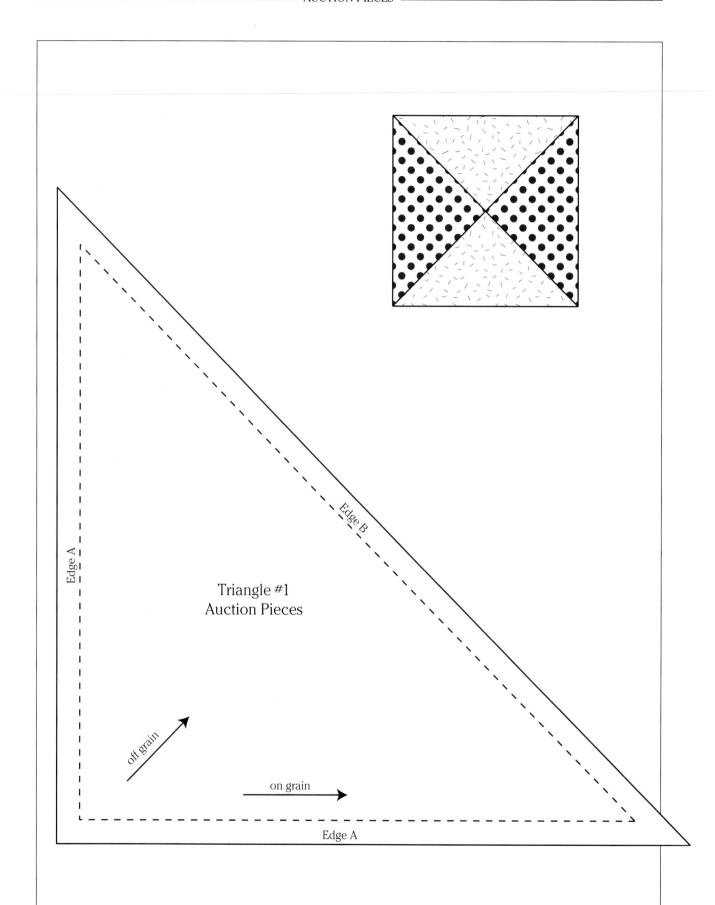

Triangle #1
Auction Pieces

Edge A

Edge B

off grain

on grain

Edge A

STARRY STARRY TIES

85" x 85", by June Barnes, 1994,
machine pieced and machine quilted, quilt raffled,
raising over £1,000 for Save the Children.

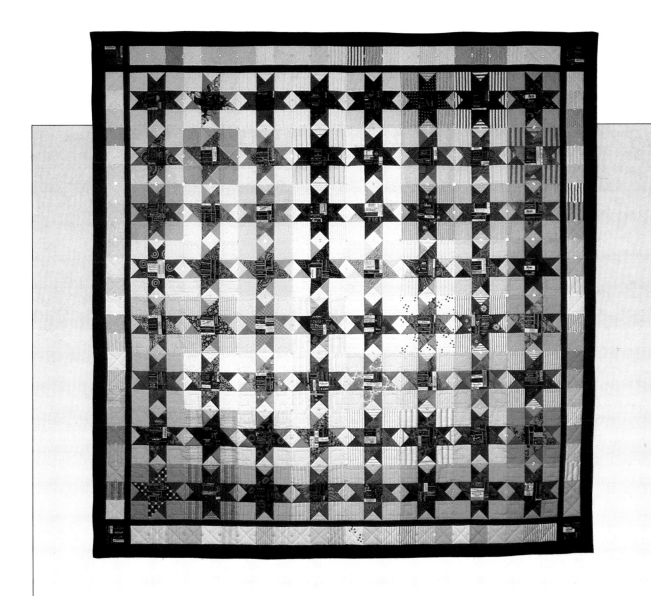

From East Sussex, England, June collects neckties and shirting fabrics for the quilts she makes to raffle for charities. She has a most extensive tie collection (over 7000) which she amassed through charity shops, jumble sales, and donations. Through June's efforts, her favorite charities have been the beneficiaries of monies brought in by her dedicated efforts.

For STARRY STARRY TIES, June used a product available in UK, Ultra-Soft Iron-On Vilene, which she used on both ties and shirting background fabrics. Independently, she and I have found that iron-on interfacing achieves beautiful results.

The quilt is made up of 64 – 9" Double Friendship Star blocks with a 6½" pieced border. Each block contains two ties (one plain and one patterned) and one shirting fabric. The quilt is constructed in four sections to make machine quilting easier.

Techniques

Iron-on interfacing
Templates or half-square triangles
Embellishment with buttons and labels
Quilted in sections

FOR THE STARRY STARRY TIES QUILT

Fabric	# of Ties or shirts	Yardage	Template	# to Cut
Plain ties	64		C	4 each
Patterned ties	64		B	4 each
Shirts	64		C	4 each
			A	7 each of 36 shirts
			A	6 each of 28 shirts
Backing: Shirting fabric or cotton		14" x 85"		2 strips 72½" x 7"
				2 strips 85" x 7"
Shirting squares (from the 64shirts)			9½" x 9½"	1 square each
Vilene® or PELLON®		7½ –8 yards	A	420
			B	256
			C	512
Border: Black cotton		2½ yards		I: 2 strips 72½" x 1½"
				II: 4 strips 3½" x 1½"
				III: 2 strips 80½" x 1½"
				IV: 2 strips 80½" x 3"
				V: 2 strips 85" x 3"
Backing		14" x 85"		2 strips 72½" x 7"
				2 strips 85" x 7"
Labels from ties				
150-160 shirt buttons				
Wadding (batting)		90" x 90"		

Sturdy template material to be used with rotary cutter.

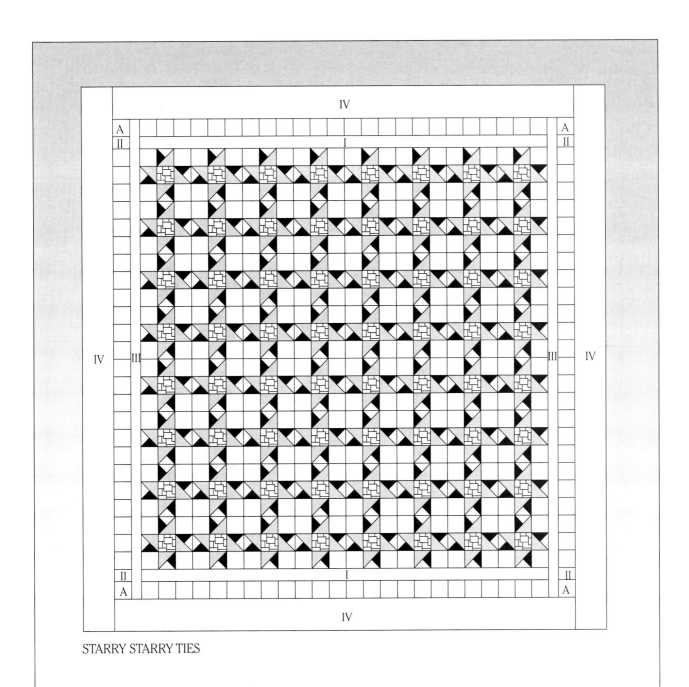

STARRY STARRY TIES

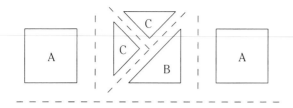

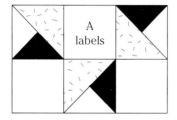

Fig. 85

extra batting

Fig. 86

Preparation

- Sort the tie fabrics into 64 coordinated pairs.
- Iron on interfacing to all shirt and tie pieces (except backing squares and fabrics). After ironing, true up each piece of fabric with its template. June cautions not to rely on the Vilene® shape as it occasionally stretches/distorts with ironing.
- For each block, attach labels in a crazy patchwork fashion, to one shirting square which will go in the center of the star. Use a piece of scrap paper underneath the fabric to avoid puckering, stitching labels around the edges using a satin stitch.

Sewing

- Lay out the block pieces and stitch together as follows (Fig. 85).
- Press the seams open.
- Pin the completed block to a matching 9½" square of shirting (for backing) and set aside.
- Construct all 64 blocks in this manner.
- Lay out the blocks in a pleasing arrangement in four 4 x 4 block sections.
- Sew the blocks together.
- Press seams open.

Making the Top / Wadding (Batting) / Backing Sandwich

- Carefully arrange the 9½" x 9½" backing squares of shirting to correspond with the 4 x 4 block sections.
- Stitch the backing shirting squares together in 4 x 4 block sections.
- Press the seams open.
- Cut the wadding into four pieces 45" x 45" each.
- Sandwich the quilt top, wadding, and backing for each of the four sections of the quilt, leaving 7" extra allowance for the borders as indicated in Fig. 86.
- Secure the quilt sandwich with safety pins.

Quilting

Machine quilt the four separate sections in-the-ditch, outlining the stars. Do not quilt to the outside edges. (Quilting will be completed when the four sections are joined.) Additional quilting may be added (see Fig. 87).

Joining the Sections

- Pin the top two sections of the quilt top only together and stitch.
- Press seams open.
- Trim the wadding to meet, not overlap.
- Join the wadding edges by hand with a herringbone stitch (Fig. 88).
- Pin and stitch the backing sections in place, by hand.
- Complete the quilting along the joined lines.
- Join the bottom two sections as above.
- Quilt.
- Join the top section to the bottom section as above.
- Quilt. All four sections will be joined and quilted, leaving the edges free (Fig. 89).

Borders

- Layout the shirting fabrics into four strips of 24 squares each.
- Join together.
- Press seams open.
- Cover the four remaining shirt pieces (A) with labels as described earlier in the Preparation section. These will be corner blocks for the inner lattice.
- Join the two borders as follows: label block (A) + one black strip (II) + one strip of 24 shirt squares + one black strip (II) + one label block (A). Press fabrics towards black. Set aside (Fig. 90).
- Stitch a black strip (I) to the top and bottom of the quilt top, carefully keeping the wadding/batting and backing free. Press towards black (Fig. 91, page 116).

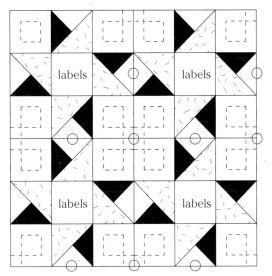

Fig. 87

wadding
wadding — stitches through wadding
— stitches front of wadding

Fig. 88

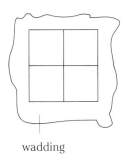

wadding

Fig. 89

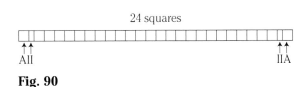

24 squares

AII   IIA

Fig. 90

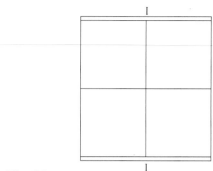

Fig. 91

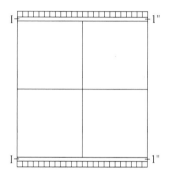

Fig. 92

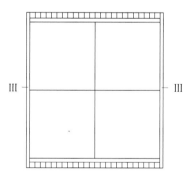

Fig. 93

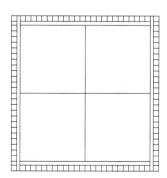

Fig. 94

- Stitch the two remaining shirting strips to the top and bottom of the quilt. Press towards black (Fig. 92).
- Stitch black strips (III) to the sides of the quilt. Press towards black (Fig. 93).
- Stitch the pieced border strips (fifth step) to the sides of the quilt. Press to black (Fig. 94).
- Stitch black strips (IV) to the top and bottom of the quilt. Press towards black.
- Stitch black strips (V) to the sides of the quilt. Press towards black.

Finishing the Backing

There should be 7" of wadding all around the edges of the quilt top.

- Stitch 7" x 72½" backing strips to the top and bottom of the quilt backing. Press the backing towards the border.
- Stitch the 7" x 85" backing strips to the sides of the quilt backing. Press towards border.

Completing the Quilt

- Sandwich the border sections, holding the layers together with safety pins.
- Machine quilt the border as indicated in Fig. 95.
- Complete the quilting on the outside edges of the quilt.
- Bind with black bias.
- Stitch buttons onto the quilt as indicated by circles on the diagram.

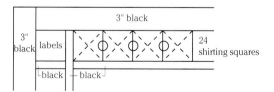

Fig. 95

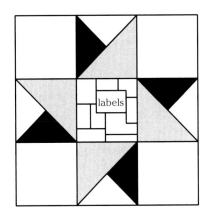

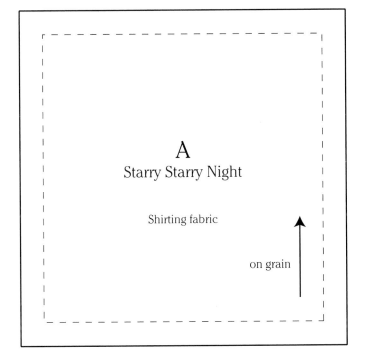

A
Starry Starry Night

Shirting fabric

on grain

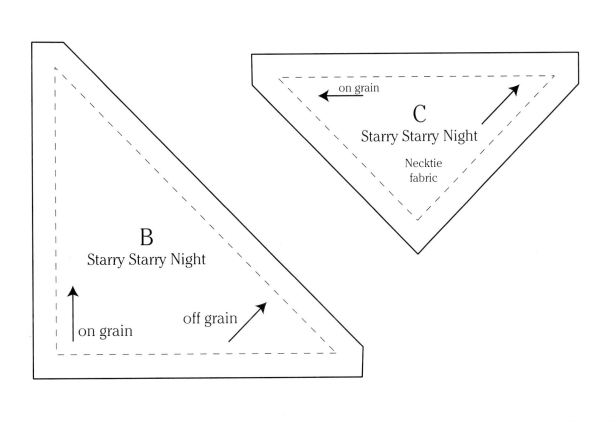

B
Starry Starry Night

on grain

off grain

C
Starry Starry Night

on grain

Necktie
fabric

ALL TIED UP / GOOSE GRIDLOCK

98" x 104", by Judy Dales, 1995,
machine pieced and hand quilted, in the Dales collection.

Judy has developed a teaching concept which she calls Colorflow. It allows you to create an abstract design using a large variety of fabrics, working intuitively with the color. The painterly look achieved with Colorflow lends itself beautifully to her collection of 100% cotton tie scraps from friend Sue Rodger's necktie factory source.

Judy worked with 50 different dark tie fabrics and over 200 different light fabrics. The design, which was created on graph paper, combines Pinwheels and Flying Geese motifs in an abstract, loose manner. Each large triangle in the pattern is really two half-square triangles cut from the same fabric, which makes the piecing much simpler.

The background areas of the design are pieced from 2¾" squares. Some of the pieces could be combined into larger templates, but Judy thinks it is more interesting to keep the pieces small so that a lot of different fabrics can be used, adding great interest to the background.

Techniques

Half-square triangles (new method)
Templates with seam allowance
Traditional piecing
Flannel board layout

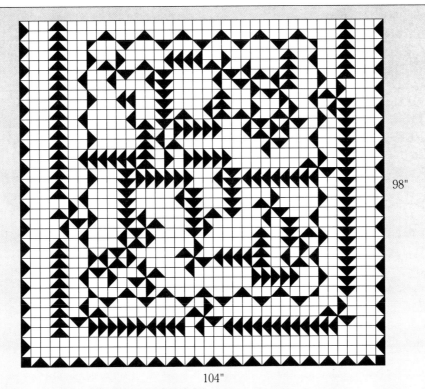

98"

104"

ALL TIED UP / GOOSE GRIDLOCK

FOR THE ALL TIED UP / GOOSE GRIDLOCK QUILT

Fabric	# of Ties	Yardage	Template	# to Cut
Dark ties	30		B	720 (24 each)
Background: 8 pieces		1⅛ yards each	B	720 (90 each)
			A	560 (70 each)
Backing		7½ yards		
Binding		⅝ yard		

The fabric requirements list the minimum of ties and background fabrics needed to make this quilt. For this quilt, the more fabric, the more interesting the quilt. For the background, Judy suggests buying more pieces with less yardage, e.g., instead of buying 1 yard of fabric, buy 4 pieces of ¼ yard each.

Cutting

Judy's unique method of cutting triangles and squares works fine on most neckties. If your necktie is too narrow in the center, cut up to that portion. Piece some of your leftover necktie fabric to make the remaining narrow section the required width. Remember, ties already have seams, so joining pieces is perfectly acceptable.

There are also templates at the end of this chapter, if you have only small scraps and cannot use the half-square triangle method.

You may want to cut more pieces than you need so you can play around with your fabric choices in ties and background.

The following instructions are general as you may have made your own design. If using Judy's layout, please refer to the amounts needed in the chart page 119.

Background

Cut each piece of background fabric into 11 strips 3¼" wide. Then cut the strips into squares and triangles as follows.

Squares

Cut 3¼" x 3¼" background squares from the strips. Each strip will yield 12 squares.

Triangles

Cut a paper Template B. Tape it on the back of your ruler with the long bias edge of the triangle along the cutting edge of the ruler. Cut the 3¼" strips into 4" rectangles. Position the ruler so that the 90 degree angle of the template matches one 90 degree corner of the rectangle. Cut along the cutting edge to divide the rectangle into triangles (Fig. 96).

Neckties

For wide ties, cut 3¼" strips as above and cut into triangles. For scraps, cut 720 triangles from Template B.

Stitching Sequence

- Layout all the squares and triangles according to your diagram.
- Two contrasting triangles can be joined. Two of these squares can then be joined to form one "flying goose" unit (Fig 97).
- Two triangles similar in color or value can be joined to form squares as shown (Fig 98).
- Use these square and triangle units as building blocks for your design.
- After you have finished the new design, sew the pieces together, with all the triangles together first.

Fig. 97

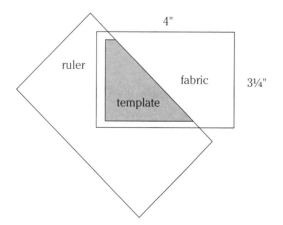

Fig. 96

Fig. 98

- Develop a system for keeping track of the direction of the seams and the placement of the light and dark triangles. Judy picks up the light triangle first and flips it over onto the dark triangle. Then she puts a pin in the place where the light triangle used to be, running parallel to the seam line (Fig. 99).
- Sew the seams, pressing seam allowance toward the dark triangles. When bringing a unit back to the flannel board, the pin will tell you which direction the seam runs and which side of the patch is light. This system enables you to keep track of the triangle units so you don't forget what goes where.
- Sew the quilt together by rows, keeping the pieces in the proper order.
- Press these seams in alternate directions.

Finishing

- Press the finished quilt top.
- Baste the quilt top, batting, and backing together.
- Quilt as desired.
- Bind the quilt.

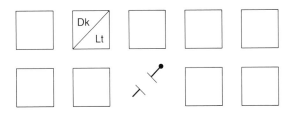

Fig. 99

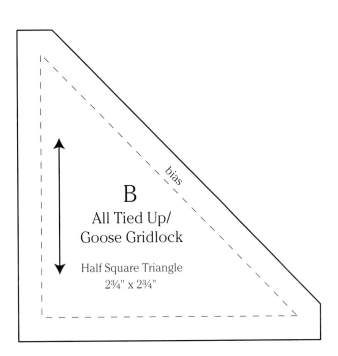

B
All Tied Up/
Goose Gridlock

Half Square Triangle
2¾" x 2¾"

FREEDOM

80" x 96", by Janet Elwin, ©1995,
machine pieced and machine quilted, in the Elwin collection.

Quiltmakers cannot deny that neckties and Log Cabin blocks just naturally go together. My first intention was to make a wallhanging, but I changed my original 36 block all necktie Log Cabin into quite the project. It turned out to be a sampling of three approaches all combined in one.

"Freedom" refers to the freedom of the employees at Hewlett-Packard (the company Bud works for) to come to work on Fridays in casual dress.

Techniques

Foundation piecing on muslin
Embellishments with labels and buttons

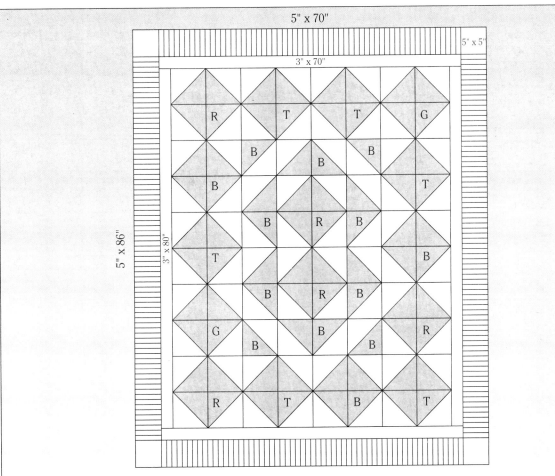

FREEDOM

There are four different sturdy polyester (no silk or lightweight) fabric sections making up FREEDOM:

- Section I – 8 blocks, gray and red ties
- Section II – 16 blocks, blue ties and blue shirting fabric
- Section III – 24 blocks, variety of ties and yellow shirting fabrics

- Section IV – 32 blocks, all ties for both light and dark sides of the blocks

Each section could be a complete project in itself and make a lovely wallhanging, but I feel that once you have started, you will want to work on.

The sewing technique is the same for the blocks in each section, but the fabric use is different. The easiest blocks to make were in Section I,

R	R	T	T	T	T	G	G
R	R	T	T	T	T	G	G
B	B	B	B	B	B	T	T
B	B	B	R	R	B	T	T
T	T	B	R	R	B	B	B
T	T	B	R	R	B	B	B
G	G	B	R	R	B	R	R
G	G	B	B	B	B	R	R
R	R	T	T	B	B	T	T
R	R	T	T	B	B	T	T

R – red center
B – blue center
T – tan center
G – green center

Fig. 100

Section I – red/gray
Section II – blue ties/blue shirting
Section III – variety ties/shirting
Section IV – ties light and dark

Fig. 101

using only two ties in each block, one light and one dark. The most challenging were the all tie combinations in Section IV.

I recommend sewing this quilt on fabric foundations as all the tie and shirting fabrics are cut on the bias.

Fabrics

The Log Cabin pattern relies on high contrast between light and dark fabrics to show the design. When selecting ties for this project, look for solids, small prints, narrow strips with very little contrast, overall patterns with little contrast, and small patterned ties. Ties with wide contrasting stripes, and large patterns and prints won't work well for this quilt.

Even with as many ties as I had, I found it difficult to get enough really light ones I needed for contrast. I used many ties on the reverse side which was a real help, but still I ripped out as many blocks as I put together.

Color Arrangement

There are as many ways to arrange a Log Cabin as there are quilters. This is how the fabrics have been arranged in this project (Figs. 100 and 101).

Section I – There are eight blocks in Section I. For one block cut the center square and all red logs from one red tie. Use one gray tie for all the light logs. Change to a different red/gray combination for each of the remaining seven blocks.

Sections II and III – For each block the light logs are from three shirting fabrics, and the centers and dark logs are from five coordinated dark neckties.

Section IV – For each block the centers and all the dark logs are from five coordinated dark ties. The light logs are from three light ties.

The fabrics are arranged in the following chart for the light and dark sides of the Log Cabin block. Note that for some of the light sides, shirting is used and for others light ties.

FOR THE LOG CABIN BLOCK

Light Side	Fabric	Dark Side	Fabric
Logs #2 and #3	Shirting #1 or light tie	Centers: red, tan, green, or blue	Tie 1
Logs #6 and #7	Shirting #2 or light tie	Log #1	Dark Tie 2
Logs #10 and #11	Shirting #3 or light tie	Logs #4 and #5	Dark Tie 3
		Logs #8 and #9	Dark Tie 4
		Log #12	Dark Tie 5

Fabric requirements in the chart below are given by sections, with the very least amount of neckties required. If you have a huge supply of ties, cut at least three times the amounts given in order to have a good mix to choose from.

FOR THE FREEDOM QUILT – BY SECTIONS

Fabric	# of Ties	Yardage	# to Cut
SECTION I – 8 Blocks			
Neckties	8 gray		1 strip 2" wide each
Neckties	8 red		1 strip 2" wide each
Neckties	1 red		8 – 3" squares
SECTION II – 16 Blocks			
Neckties	16 blue		1 strip 2" wide each
Necktie	1 blue		16 – 3" squares
Shirting #1		⅜ yard	32 pieces*
Shirting #2		½ yard	32 pieces*
Shirting #3		¾ yard	32 pieces*
SECTION III – 24 Blocks			
Neckties	4 red/blue		1 strip 2" wide each
Neckties	5 purple		1 strip 2" wide each
Neckties	7 brown		1 strip 2" wide each
Neckties	8 blue		1 strip 2" wide each
Neckties	1 tan		11 – 3" squares
Necktie	1 green		3 – 3" squares
Necktie	1 blue		6 – 3" squares
Necktie	1 red		4 – 3" squares
Shirting #1		½ yard	48 pieces*
Shirting #2		¾ yard	48 pieces*
Shirting #3		1⅛ yards	48 pieces*

FOR THE FREEDOM QUILT – BY SECTIONS

Fabric	# of Ties	Yardage	# to Cut
SECTION IV – 32 Blocks			
Neckties (lights)	32 pink, beige, and gray		1 strip 2" wide each
Neckties (dark)	5 red		1 strip 2" wide each
Neckties (dark)	7 purple		1 strip 2" wide each
Neckties (dark)	9 brown		1 strip 2" wide each
Neckties (dark)	9 green		1 strip 2" wide each
Neckties (dark)	11 blue		1 strip 2" wide each
Neckties (dark)	1 red		8 – 3" squares
Neckties (dark)	1 tan		12 – 3" squares
Neckties (dark)	1 green		5 – 3" squares
Neckties (dark)	1 blue		6 – 3" squares
Label Border and Corners: Wool gray tweed**		⅞ yard	2 strips 3½" x 70½"
			2 strips 3½" x 80½"
			4 squares 5½" x 5½"
Strip Border: Neckties	use leftovers		150 – 2" x 6" strips of ties
Foundation Squares: Muslin***		4 yards	80 – 9" squares
Foundation for Strip Border: Muslin***			2 strips 6" x 72"
Binding: neckties	approx. 7		stitch 2" strips together to
			make a 360" strip
Backing: Cotton or shirting		5¼ yards	
Labels	300 labels		
Buttons	375 buttons		

* See cutting instructions on page 127.

** You could use a pair of men's dark gray tweed slacks at least 32" long.

*** If you want to hand quilt, substitute a very fine lawn or lightweight blend fabric for the muslin.

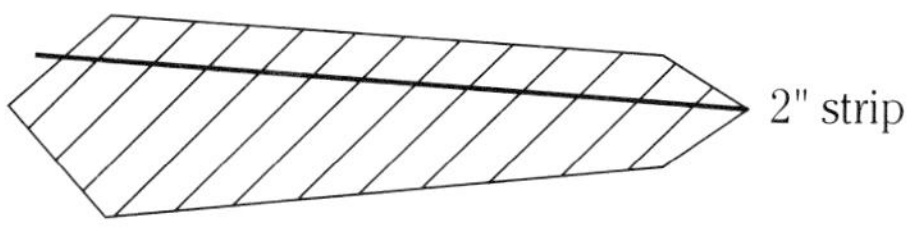

Fig. 102

2" strip

Cutting

Logs from Necktie Fabrics

Cut 2" strips (logs) from the sides of the ties. Then cut the remaining ties into strips for the binding and into 6" strips to be used for the strip border. The 2" wide strips for the logs leave ample seam allowance (Fig. 102).

Centers

Each tie yields approximately 20 – 3" squares for the centers. The layout diagram, Fig. 100, page 124, is marked to show what colors are used for the centers of each block. To cut the centers all the same color, use four similar color ties and cut 80 – 3" squares.

Logs from Shirting Fabrics

To keep in the spirit of cutting off-grain, follow these diagrams for cutting shirting fabrics:

SHIRTING FABRIC #1

Cut fabric into 4" strips. Cut three strips for Section II and four strips for Section III. Starting from a corner of a strip, cut 45° 2" diagonal strips. Each row yields 12 strips (Fig 103).

SHIRTING FABRIC #2

Cut fabric into 6" strips. Cut three strips for Section II and four strips for Section III. Starting from a corner of a strip, cut 45° 2" diagonal strips (Fig. 104).

SHIRTING FABRIC #3

Cut fabric into 8" strips. Cut three strips for Section II and five strips for Section III. Starting from a corner of a strip, cut 45° 2" diagonal strips (Fig. 105).

Foundation Fabric

Cut 80 – 9" foundation squares. Cut two 6" x 72" strips and two 6" x 88" strips for the strip border. It's OK to piece the border foundation strips.

Marking the Foundation Pieces

Foundation Pieces for Strip Borders

Across the 6" width of the fabric, mark sewing lines, starting in ½", then every 1", ending with ½" (Fig. 106).

Foundation Squares

Use a light box and a ruler to trace the pattern onto each 9" square, adding ½" seam allowance

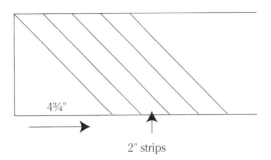

Fig. 103

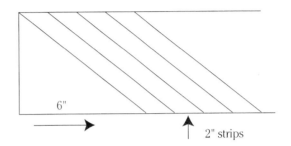

Fig. 104

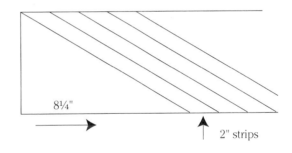

Fig. 105

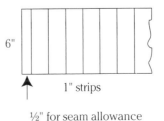

Fig. 106

all around. This ½" seam allowance allows for any shrinkage in sewing. OR

Pin three foundation squares together with carbon paper between them. Mark as before. Do this in front of the TV news. Fortunately, it doesn't take as long as it sounds.

Sewing Sequence

If this *whole* project seems overwhelming, break it down by sections. Sections I is a snap and once you see how easy the piecing is, you will want to continue. Make 72 Log Cabin blocks.

Here are some brief sewing instructions. Reread Chapter 2 for more information on foundation piecing.

- Sew the logs to the foundation square, following the numbered sequence.
- Press after stitching each log. If having an iron and pad beside your sewing machine is impossible, use flowerhead pins and pin each log in place. Leave the pin in place until the log is stitched. Then press each block after all the logs are stitched.
- Because I wasn't hand quilting, I didn't trim seam allowances to ¼" unless the dark showed through to the light.
- Staystitch ¼" from the outside edge of the muslin.
- Trim each finished Log Cabin block to 8½" x 8½".

Assembling the Blocks

- Lay out all the blocks according to the diagram.
- Stitch the blocks together in rows, 8 blocks per row.
- Stitch the 10 rows together, alternating the direction of pressing the seams in each row.

Label Border and Corners

If you use a pair of men's wool slacks, machine wash wool on a gentle cycle, line dry, and iron. Cut into strips and stitch together to make two 3½" x 70½" strips and two 3½" x 80½" strips. Cut four corner squares 5½" x 5½".

- Scatter labels across the border strips and corner squares.
- Zigzag around the edges of the labels.
- Press.

Strip Border

- Stitch the 6" x 2" tie strips onto the muslin foundation strips. These tie strips are the ones leftover from cutting the logs for the blocks.
- Press.
- After sewing all the small tie strips onto the foundation strips, trim the borders. The side strips should measure 5½" x 86½". The top and bottom strips should measure 5½" x 70½".

Final Assembly

- Stitch the corner blocks on each end of the top and bottom strips and press the seams.
- Pin and stitch the wool label borders to the quilt and press the seams.
- Pin and stitch the strip borders to the quilt and press the seams.
- Baste the finished quilt top to the batting and backing. Because of the weight of the ties and muslin foundations, the quilt will be heavy. I recommend using a lightweight Hobbs Thermore® batting.
- Quilt in-the-ditch except on the label borders.
- Machine stitch buttons along the label borders through all the layers.
- Bind the quilt with necktie fabric.

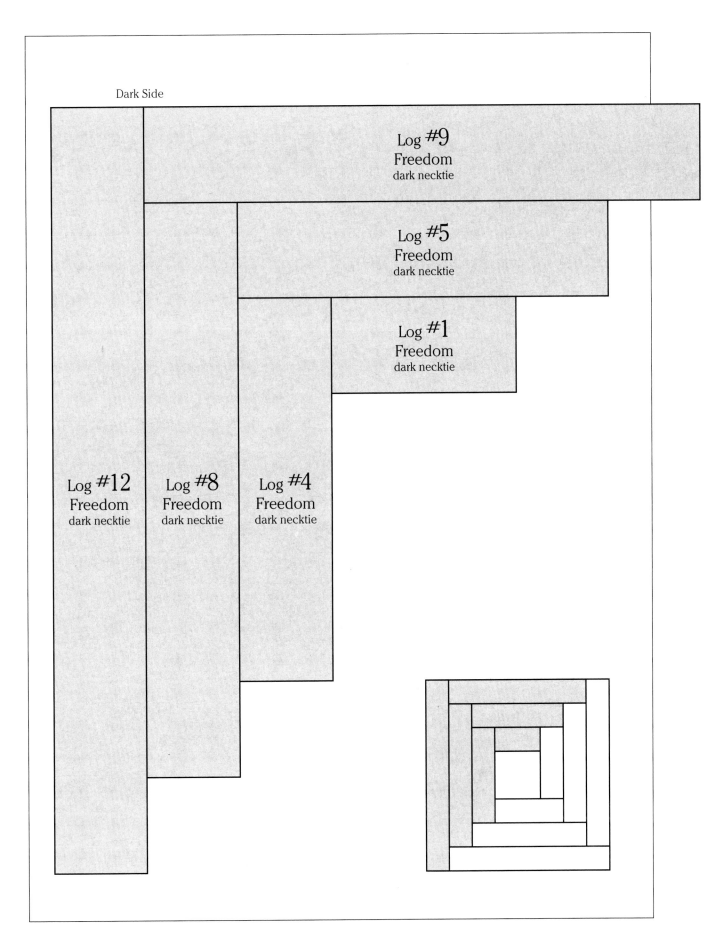

Dark Side

Log #9
Freedom
dark necktie

Log #5
Freedom
dark necktie

Log #1
Freedom
dark necktie

Log #12
Freedom
dark necktie

Log #8
Freedom
dark necktie

Log #4
Freedom
dark necktie

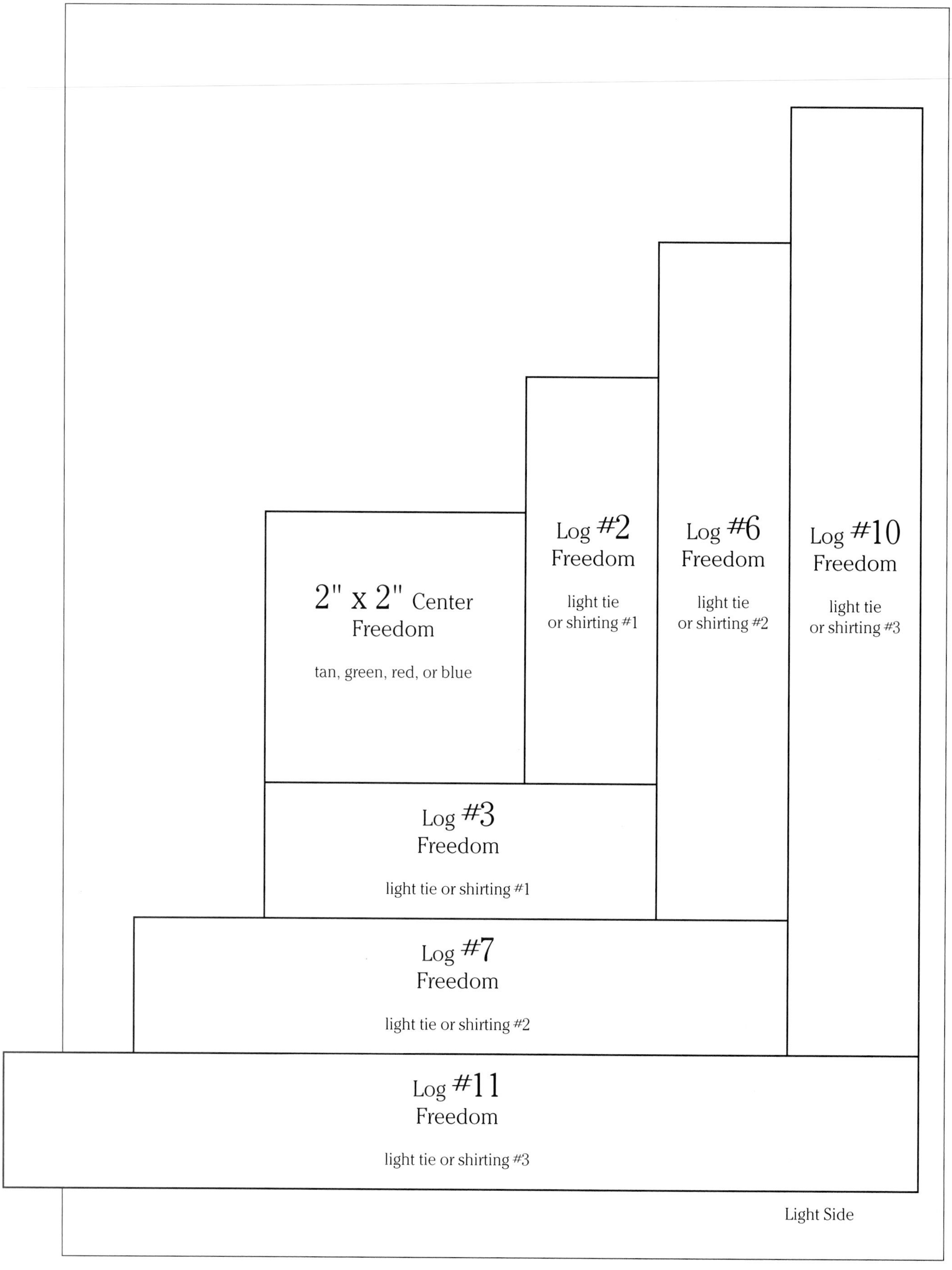

2" x 2" Center
Freedom

tan, green, red, or blue

Log #2
Freedom

light tie
or shirting #1

Log #6
Freedom

light tie
or shirting #2

Log #10
Freedom

light tie
or shirting #3

Log #3
Freedom

light tie or shirting #1

Log #7
Freedom

light tie or shirting #2

Log #11
Freedom

light tie or shirting #3

Light Side

Chapter

7

Where Do We Go From Here?

BONDED APPLIQUÉ HANDBAG

Laura Mooers Woods, 1995,
appliquéd.

In my youth, of course, I never dreamed that I would grow up recycling neckties for a living, but here I am. I started off with a very simple project, my necktie skirt, and now all these years later I find myself making quilts, wallhangings, and now back to clothing again – a pleasant cycle that will continue, always returning to clothing, some patchwork and some not, at the end of projects.

Garments can be made fairly quickly. Even patchwork clothing is fast compared to some quilts. Vowing not to get into clothing in this book because of the size of the pattern pieces, I couldn't help myself. In this chapter there are several projects: a fabulous evening bag by Laura Mooers Woods, a recycled man's shirt, a skirt from ties, a crazy patch holiday jacket, and even some recycled ties.

Laura creates the most wonderful handbags from bits and pieces of tie fabrics, dressy fabrics, cottons, threads, ribbons, yarns, etc. For those of you who can't bear to part with snippets of treasured fabrics and embellishments, this is the project for you.

Techniques

Machine sewing

Creative embellishment using fusible fabric and bits and pieces

FOR THE BONDED APPLIQUÉ HANDBAG

Fabric	# to Cut
Handbag fabric	10" x 14"* and 14" x 18"
Interfacing (non-woven, not iron-on)	8" x 12" and 14" x 18"
Lining	8" x 12" and 14" x 18"
Lining or other fabric for optional inside pocket	8" x 9"
Bridal illusion net	12" x 16"
Fusible web	10" x 14" (leave the paper)

*This piece is to create your bonded appliqué fabric. It will be trimmed to 8" x 12" later.

Supplies

- Bits and pieces of leftover tie fabrics
- ¾ yard fabric for the handbag fabric
- ¾ to 1 yard lining – nice print
- ¾ to 1 yard of fusible web such as Wonder Under, Heat and Bond or Fine Fuse
- ¾ yard medium weight interfacing – *Not Iron-on!*
- ½ yard bridal illusion net in a color to match the background fabric or to contrast for a different effect. (Bridal illusion is the fine net used for veils, not standard nylon net.)
- Freezer paper
- Deli-wrap paper (thin lightly waxed paper) available from restaurant supply companies or try your local deli
- Scraps of yarn, lace, ribbon floss, embroidery threads, tissue lame fabric*

- Thread to match the background fabric
- Metallic thread to complement your embellishment (you may want to use a size 14 or 16 sewing machine needle for this or a special needle designed for metallic thread)
  *Mail order sources: Clotilde and Keepsake Quilting (see Resources at the end of this book)

Preparation

- Cut the following according to the chart above.
- Place a piece of deli-wrap paper on your ironing board to protect it. Lay the fusible web, paper side up, on the right side of your 10" x 14" handbag fabric. The right sides will be together away from the iron. Place on the ironing board with the fusible web paper on top. Fuse the web to

the fabric using a dry iron set for wool or cotton. Hold the iron in place for five seconds. Then lift the iron and fuse the next area. Continue to lift and press until the whole piece is fused.

- Let the fabric cool. Then remove the paper backing, trying not to tear it. Save the paper for later. Return your fused fabric to the ironing board, still using the deli-wrap paper to protect the ironing board.

Playtime
Creating Bonded Appliqué Fabric

- *Now it is finally time to play!* You may carefully plan a composition or create using the "toss a handful" technique. Start adding items of your choice to embellish the handbag. Some suggestions are:
  - ‣ Small snips of tie fabrics
  - ‣ Yarns
  - ‣ Shredded pieces of lamé
  - ‣ Twirls of ribbon floss
  - ‣ Lace
  - ‣ Ribbons
  - ‣ Fancy and not so fancy thread
- When you like your creation, *Stop!* Lay the piece of bridal illusion net over your creation. Top this creation with the paper backing you saved from the fusible web.
- Fuse the layers in place using the same method for fusing the fusible web. Press for five seconds, lift the iron, and press the next area. Be careful not to scorch your fabric or your embellishments.
- Remove the top layer of paper and throw it away.
- Lay a piece of deli-wrap paper over the top and fuse again. Repeat this step until all traces of fusible web are removed. Because the excess web may be stick *do not reuse this paper for ironing or fusing.*

Decorative Stitching on the Bonded Appliqué Fabric

- With the deli-wrap paper still underneath, stitch through all the layers in a stitch pattern of your choice using a contrasting thread or a decorative thread. On the Pfaff Creative 7550, stitches #126, 152, or 181 would look nice.
- Trim the piece down to 8" x 12".
- Remove all the paper that you can.

Assemble

- Pin the bonded appliqué fabric and the 8" x 12" lining fabric right sides together. Lay the interfacing on top (Fig. 107).
- Sew three sides using a ½" seam allowance, leaving one long edge open.
- Trim the seams to a scant ¼", and trim the corners diagonally (Fig. 108).
- Turn the right sides out, paying special attention to the corners. Be gentle.
- Place the 14" x 18" piece of interfacing on the wrong side of the 14" x 18" bag fabric. Fold this in half to form a 9" x 14" rectangle. Sew the side seams together using a ½" seam allowance, leaving the third side open (Fig. 109).
- If you want an inside pocket, add it now. Using the 8" x 9" piece of fabric, fold it in half, right sides together. Stitch around the three sides, leaving a small opening for turning. Turn the pocket right side out and press. Center the pocket on the bag lining 1½" from the top edge and approximately 3½" from each side. Top stitch the pocket in place with two rows of straight stitching or one row of strong or heavily decorative stitching (Fig. 110).
- Fold the 14" x 18" rectangle of lining fabric in half to form a 9" x 14" rectangle. Stitch the two ends using a ½" seam, leaving the third side open (Fig. 111).

- On the wrong side of the lining, pull the corners out and measure 1½" from the tip of the corner and draw a line. Stitch on this line. Repeat this corner treatment step on the outside fabric. Leave the lining wrong side out (Fig. 112).
- Turn the handbag right side out. Center the optional front flap along one long edge of the handbag. This should be about 1" from the side seams. Sew the flap in place using a ¼" seam allowance.
- Insert the handbag into the lining with right sides together. Attach the optional strap (see following instructions) if you are adding one. Pin all the way around the top edge. The pocket goes on the side with the flap. Stitch as pinned, using a ½" seam allowance and leaving a 5" opening on the front edge of the bag.
- Turn the bag right side out using the opening. Press the bag, paying special attention to the edges. Hand stitch the opening closed using matching thread.

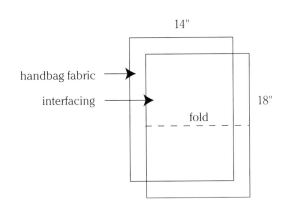

Fig. 109

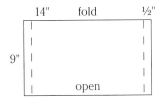

Fig. 110

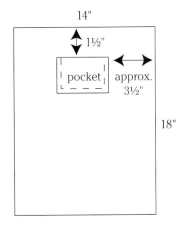

Fig. 111

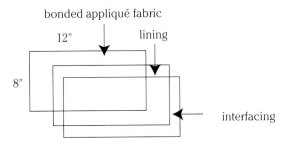

Fig. 107

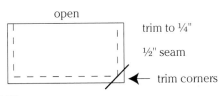

Fig. 108

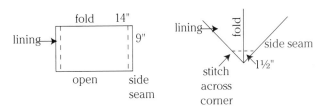

Fig. 112

Optional Strap

Braid or knot several pieces of cording or yarn together. Pin the ends of the strap to the sides of the bag and stitch in place when the top edge is stitched.

OR

Sew the strap by hand onto the outside of the handbag.

Optional Front Flap

Be creative in cutting the front flap. It doesn't have to be a rectangular shape. Here are a couple of suggestions see Fig. 113.

To make these shapes, cut a paper pattern by eye, or fold a piece of paper in half and cut a symmetrical design.

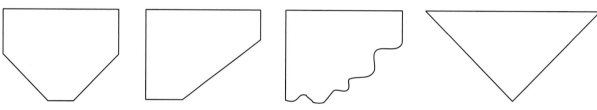

Fig. 113

BUD'S SHIRT AND TIE(S)

Janet Elwin, 1995,
machine stitched.

When I was hunting around for shirting fabrics for a project, I found several shirts Bud had contributed to the "cause." There were three that coordinated very well, so for once I decided to recycle them to see what happened. Here are the results of the recycling. If you don't have three coordinating shirts to try this, just buy a commercial pattern and have a go at it. There are also directions for making a recycled tie to go with the recycled shirt.

The beauty of doing this is that you don't have to do any tailoring. All the picky parts – collar, shirt facings, and sleeve facings – will be intact from your creative gleanings.

Fortunately Bud has a very good sense of humor. Also, I am always coming up with something new and different to wear and that has rubbed off on Bud. He wears his recycled shirt to work and play and has received good natured comments regarding his latest fashion statement.

Techniques

Straight sewing "The Easy Way Out"
or use a commercial men's shirt pattern

FOR BUD'S SHIRT

Fabric	# of Shirts
Shirt #1	1
Shirt #2	1
Shirt #3	1

*The shirts should be the same size. Color coordinate the fabrics.

Recycled Shirt

Preparation

- Very carefully take apart Shirt #1, keeping intact the right front, back facing, collar and left buttonhole facing.
- Take apart Shirt #2, saving the back and left front.
- Take apart Shirt #3, saving the sleeves.

(Re)assemble

- Pin the back of Shirt #2 to the back facing of Shirt #1. Topstitch in place.
- Pin the left front of Shirt #2 to the Shirt #1 back facing and buttonhole facing. Topstitch in place.
- Stitch in the sleeves from Shirt #3. Zigzag the edges and then topstitch ⅜" away from the seam through all thicknesses of fabric.
- Zigzag all raw edges of all the other seams.

Recycled Tie

Is your husband bored with the same old ties? He'll never complain again when you make him this custom revamped tie.

- Look over some of your ties and set aside a really nice subtle patterned or plain tie. Take apart the tie and save the lining.
- Make a paper pattern of this tie and facing. Take note of how it was sewn together.
- From your stash of ties, pick out a tie to coordinate with the first tie.
- Most striped ties have all stripes the same width (boring). Try making stripes of varying width to add some interest and a personal touch to the tie. Add a new stripe to the tie as follows.
- Remove a 1" strip along the diagonal of a plain tie. Cut a 2" strip along the diagonal, the "inset piece," of a coordinating tie. Cut the inset piece 1" wider than the piece removed (Fig. 114).

- Stitch in the inset piece along the diagonal. Make as many or as few stripes as wide or narrow as you wish. It isn't necessary to change the stripes on the entire tie. Starting from the wide end, measure from the tip up about 25". The rest of the tie doesn't show.
- After you have pieced the tie, press the seams.
- Pin on the paper pattern and recut if necessary.
- Reassemble the tie using the original lining and facings.

Fig. 114

Another Tie Option

Some ties I see on the market today in 1996 have horizontal patterns. Update an old tie by creating your own new horizontal tie (Fig. 115).

To be really creative, you might try a simple quilt pattern as follows (Fig. 116).

Fig. 115

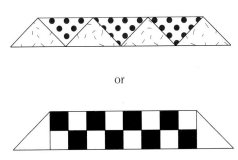

or

Fig. 116

LEA'S NECKTIE SKIRT

Janet Elwin, 1995,
machine stitched.

Making skirts out of neckties is where it all started for me. I first made a wine skirt using my Hexagon and Necktie Skirt pattern. (See Resources at the end of this book for mail-order information.)

One day my daughter Lea was home on school break and was rummaging through my ties. She came up with this skirt variation which she started and I finished.

Lea wears mini skirts which look just wonderful on her. I, on the other hand, wear my skirts almost to my ankles. You can make this exciting, quickie version in any length you wish.

Techniques

Straight sewing

FOR LEA'S SKIRT

Waist	Hips	Size	Approx. # of Ties
24"–25"	34"	8–10	15
26"–28"	37"	12–14	16
30"–32"	41"	16–18	18
34"–36"	43"	20–22	20

Preparation

- Measure your waist and hips.
- Select ties. The required numbers of ties above are approximate because of the varying width of ties. The number you need for your size may be more or less. You need enough ties for your hip measurement plus at least 4", keeping in mind that you will need fewer if you use wide ties. Also, a short skirt will requires less ties than a long one, and a snugly fitting skirt requires less ties than a full skirt.
- For the length of the finished skirt, either measure the length of your favorite skirt or measure from your waist down to the desired hem line. To this measurement, add 4" for seam allowance and waistband facing for the elastic (Fig. 117).
- To determine the hip width of the finished skirt, you must first decide if you want your skirt to fit snugly, to be slightly gathered, or to be very full. This will greatly affect how many ties you need.
- Measure the vertical distance from your

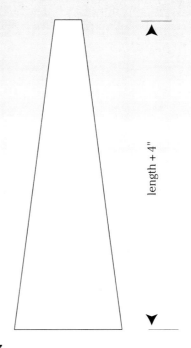

length + 4"

Fig. 117

waist to your hips. Measure down that same distance from the waist area of the tie to the hip area. Before stitching the ties together, add the hip width dimensions of all the ties selected for skirt, not including seam allowances. (Each tie will have a different width at the hip area.) See the example Fig. 118.

The number of inches the skirt is wider than your body hip width will determine how loosely or tightly the skirt fit. The waist measurement is not as critical because it will be gathered to elastic. Have at least 4" extra in the hip area for a little give, more if you want a free-swinging skirt.

Sewing

- Using a ruler, cut off the tip of each tie (Fig. 119).
- Cut the tie the length determined in third step under Preparation. If you prefer using a pattern, order Janet's necktie shirt pattern (see Resources, page 151).
- Fold the cut edges with right sides together, pin, and stitch. This is the same way of treating the tie points in the Dresden Plate quilts (see HAPPY BIRTHDAY, ALLAN, page 86) (Fig. 120).
- Turn the point to the right side. Press.
- Starting at the top edge of the tie, zigzag the sides and top of the facing of each tie (Fig. 121).
- Sew the ties together using ¼" seam allowance.
- Press all the seams to one side.
- Topstitch ⅛" along the seamline from the waistband to the bottom.
- Turn the top edge of the skirt under ¼" and machine baste.

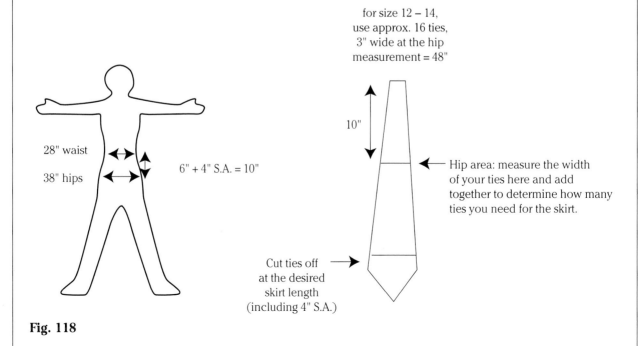

for size 12 – 14, use approx. 16 ties, 3" wide at the hip measurement = 48"

10"

Hip area: measure the width of your ties here and add together to determine how many ties you need for the skirt.

28" waist

38" hips

6" + 4" S.A. = 10"

Cut ties off at the desired skirt length (including 4" S.A.)

Fig. 118

- Make a 2" casing by folding the top edge of the skirt to the wrong side. Sew the casing all around, leaving a 3" opening.
- Measure the elastic – your waist measurement plus 2". Pin a large safety pin to one end of the elastic.
- Thread the elastic through the casing using the pin to push through the casing. Remove the pin.
- Lap the elastic over 1" and stitch the ends together. Stitch the casing opening closed.
- Hand hem the facing all around. Lea's skirt was also topstitched ½" all around the bottom edge.

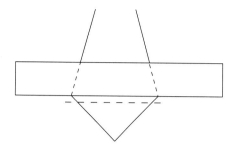

Fig. 119

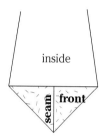

inside

seam front

Fig. 120

Fig. 121

BERGDORF'S, AGAIN

A holiday jacket,
Janet Elwin, ©1995,
machine appliquéd and machine decorated.

My neighbors, Polly and Ed McLaughlin, gave me some clothing items to recycle. Among them was a fabulous black faille dress from the 1950's from Bergdorf Goodmans and a lovely silk tie from China. Aunt Edythe contributed a silvery fabric, so with lots of hints from Eila Tegethoff who made the crazy quilt for this book, I started in making this holiday jacket.

I used a favorite out-of-date Butterick pattern.

Basically it is a vest with sleeves. Choose your favorite jacket pattern and alter the fabric requirements as needed. A simple pattern usually works best.

Techniques

Commercial pattern
Crazy quilting
Machine embroidery
Decorations

FOR BERGDORF'S, AGAIN

Fabric	# of Ties	Yardage
Black silk ties, plain, patterned and striped	10	
Muslin		2 yards
Black faille		1 yard
Silver patterned polyester		¼ yard
Lining		2 yards
Black velvet ribbon		10 yards

Decorative threads: metallic, embroidery, anything glitzy
1 gorgeous button(s), see jacket instructions.

Preparing the Pieces

- Set up your iron and ironing board next to your cutting area.
- Lay out the pattern pieces for the front, back, and sleeves of the jacket on the muslin. Cut the pieces, leaving an extra 1" all around all pieces, except if the edge of the jacket back is on a fold.
- Start with jacket back (you might get more creative as you go along and you want your best work in the front). Cut a good-sized piece of tie fabric or faille to fit in the lower left corner of the muslin. The decorative part of the jacket, not the piecing, will take up most of your time.
- With the iron on the silk setting, iron the edges ¼" under on all sides of the piece except the outer garment edges.
- Pin the piece in place.
- Cut another piece and iron under all edges under ¼". Position the piece to cover the preceding piece. Lots of these pieces will overlap. If you can keep track, only iron under the edges which will not be overlapped. However, I found it just as easy to iron under all the edges, especially if I decided to change the placement of some of the pieces.
- Continue cutting shapes and covering the entire muslin pattern piece. Be creative. Cut some with a gentle curve and some with jagged edges. Iron under the edges and pin the pieces to the muslin.
- Work on the sleeves next in the same way as the back. Mark the muslin right and left.

- The front of the jacket is the most important as it is the most visible. Now that you have a little experience with this technique, arrange more pieces to cover the jacket fronts. Mark the muslins left and right. At this point, you probably aren't too excited about the looks of the jacket. Trust me – the addition of all the embroidery will transform this "ugly duckling" into a swan.
- Measure around the jacket edge, add a couple of inches and set aside this length of velvet ribbon. Fold all the velvet ribbon in half lengthwise and baste. Use the remaining ribbon to tuck under the pinned down edges of some of the ties here and there to add a bit of texture.
- Machine stitch as close to the edges as possible along all turned-under edges using black or clear nylon thread.

Embellishing

- Now is where the fun begins, but don't be in a rush. Machine embroidery takes time. Look at different sections on the jacket. Try to find an embroidery stitch and thread that will enhance that area. Do as little or as much in each section as pleases you. I found that some threads were too thick to run through the machine so I laid them along the edges and zigzagged them in place using a matching thread.
- Iron all the pieces on the muslin side of the fabric, not the embroidered side.
- Now back to the beginning. Place all the pattern pieces on the crazy quilted muslins. Trim the muslin pieces along the pattern cutting lines as necessary.

Assembling and Finishing the Jacket

- Follow the pattern directions for jacket assembly. Before adding facings, baste the folded velvet ribbon you set aside earlier around the edge of the jacket. Sew the ribbon on the ⅝" pattern seamline, but with only ⅛" seam allowance for the ribbon.
- Lots of jackets today are unlined. If you want your jacket lined (I think evening jackets should be), just cut jacket backs, fronts and sleeves from the same pattern pieces. Stitch the lining fronts and back together. Baste, wrong sides together, to the jacket along the edges. Then add the facings. Pin in the sleeve linings and hand hem in place along the armhole seam and bottoms of the sleeves.
- Add buttonhole(s) and button(s).

Conclusion

I hate that word because it seems so final. I am hoping this book will be a beginning for you and inspire you to quilt in a new light. Working with neckties has become addictive for me as I have my mind already teeming with still another project.

I encourage you to let me know how your projects are coming along. Send pictures of what you have made from this book!

If you have devoured all the how-to information and have come up with your own projects, please share. I have a feeling that I will be working with neckties for many, many more projects to come.

For workshop – lecture information, write to:

Janet B. Elwin-Quilts Etc.
Prentiss Cove
HCR 64, Box 012
Damariscotta, Maine 04543

Biographies of Guest Quilters

JUNE BARNES

Hastings, East Sussex, United Kingdom

Starry Starry Ties, page 111.

June is a quiltmaker specializing in necktie quilts. Having made ten or more full-size quilts, all of which were raffled for charity, she is our expert tie collector. June has been featured in magazines in the United Kingdom which is where I noticed one of her fabulous charity quilts. Her recent endeavor has raised over $1,000 for Save The Children. One of June's charities had a tie collecting day which netted her 3000 ties.

RHODA COHEN

Weston, Massachusetts, and Damariscotta, Maine

Necktie Gemini, page 40.

Rhoda studied art at the Museum of Fine Arts in Boston and the DeCordova Museum in Lincoln, among others. She exhibits her work worldwide and it is in many private collections through the U.S., Europe, New Zealand, and South Africa. Rhoda lectures and teaches quilt design, color, and personal forms of expression. She recently finished a special commission for Weston Public Library, Weston, Massachusetts.

JUDY B. DALES

Boonton Township, New Jersey

All Tied Up / Goose Gridlock, page 118.

Judy is best known for her distinctive and unique color style in which she combines a wide assortment of print fabrics, including many decorator fabrics, which she has amassed during the last twenty years of her quilting career. This soft blending of colors gives her work a distinctly feminine look, and she recently has accentuated this effect by the addition of free-form curves. Judy's work has been featured in *Traditional Quiltworks, Quilting International, Creative Ideas for Living,* and *American Quilt.*

JO DIGGS

Portland, Maine

Winter Night Necktie Landscape, page 69.

Jo has cut, stitched and loved fabric since she was a child. She started exhibiting appliqué wallhangings and wearable art in New Mexico in the late 1960's. In the 1970's Jo moved to Maine where she was introduced to quilts and quilters, and she has concentrated her artistic activities in the quilt world ever since. A graduate of Wellesley College with a degree in art history and of Harvard with a master's degree in teaching, Jo's work is exhibited internationally and collected avidly. She has taught extensively in the U.S. and Canada.

JANE HALL

Raleigh, North Carolina

SILKY SCRAP PINEAPPLE, page 81.

Jane has lectured and taught quiltmaking since 1978. She is the co-author with Dixie Haywood of *Perfect Pineapples* (C&T, 1989) and *Precision Pieced Quilts Using the Foundation Method* (Chilton, 1992). Jane is intrigued by the interaction of colors in fabrics and the graphics of quilt design. She often works with traditional patterns, using a contemporary approach. She is particularly interested in Log Cabin designs and has specialized in Pineapple variations. Jane and Dixie are co-authoring a third book, *Firm Foundations: Techniques and Quilt Blocks for Precision Piecing* (AQS, 1996).

DIXIE HAYWOOD

Pensacola, Florida

TIES IN THE SKY, page 77.

Dixie started quilting in the late 1960's and has been teaching since 1974. She is the author of two books on contemporary crazy quilting, both of which have been re-printed by Dover Publications, and her articles and designs appear frequently in quilting publications. She and Jane Hall have written two books, *Perfect Pineapples* (C&T, 1989) and *Precision Pieced Quilts Using the Foundation Method* (Chilton, 1992). She says, "Many of my quilts have won awards. All of them have given me pleasure in their design, execution, and use." Dixie and Jane are co-authoring a third book, *Firm Foundations: Techniques and Quilt Blocks for Precision Piecing* (AQS, 1996).

HELEN KELLEY

Minneapolis, Minnesota

BLEST BE THE TIES, page 62.

Helen taught herself to quilt in 1946, making her wedding quilt for her marriage in 1948. People thought she was eccentric but harmless. When her oldest daughter was married in 1972, she made her a wedding quilt. (Everyone who saw the quilt, fell in love with it. Friends and family [lots of daughters] who were too shy to work on that quilt, clamored to work on the next and the next.) Helen loves experimenting with new fabrics, ideas, and techniques and wakes up each morning thinking "what if?"

MILDRED PATTERSON

Raleigh, North Carolina

FOR A LONG TALL SLEEPER, page 104.

Mildred made one quilt in 1946 for a namesake but began quilting in earnest when she retired in 1978. She says handwork is a pleasure and designing and collecting fabrics for the design are her favorite parts of creating a quilt. Mildred has made 16 large quilts, a few wallhangings, and lots of quilts for children (for a guild community project plus for great-nieces and nephews).

NORMA SCHLAGER

Brookfield, Connecticut

TAILSPIN – TIESPIN, page 36.

A former elementary school teacher, Norma came to quilting in 1976 after a lifetime of needlework and crafts and feels that she has found her niche. She specializes in "controlled" scrap quilts, which allows her to work with a myriad of fabrics. She makes her home with her husband, teenage son, two cats, and a dog.

EILA TEGETHOFF

Sabillasville, Maryland

1930'S SILK NECKTIE CRAZY QUILT, page 71.

Eila is a self-taught quilter who likes to use neckties. She has been making crazy quilt wall quilts and accessories for the past twelve years and has taught crazy quilt classes to all levels of quilters. Eila has participated in several national juried craft fairs in Maryland, Virginia, and Pennsylvania and presents a trunk show which includes vintage crazy quilts as well as her own work.

SUSANNAH VOGEL

Winthrop, Maine

AUCTION PIECES, page 107.

Susannah has enjoyed quilting for 18 years. She learned from a dear friend, Anna Banks of Liberty, Maine, who made and sold many, many beautiful quilts. Anna inspired what has been a very satisfying and relaxing part of Susannah's life.

LAURA MOOERS WOODS

Gardiner, Maine

Bonded Appliqué Handbag, page 132.

Laura is a former home economics teacher who currently teaches and exhibits her quilts and quilted clothing. She sees quilting as an adventure and it has become increasingly important in her life over the last ten years. Experimentation is for her the most satisfying and fun part of any quilting project. Her time for quilting is limited by many other demands, but she makes quilts whenever possible.

Bibliography

Beyer, Jinny. *Patchwork Patterns*. McLean, VA: EPM Publications, Inc., 1979.

Bond, Dorothy. *Crazy Quilt Stitches*. Cottage Grove, OR: self-published.

Elwin, Janet. *Creative Triangles for Quilters*. Radnor, PA: Chilton, 1995.

_____. *Hexagon Magic*. McLean, VA: EPM Publications, Inc., 1985, 1988.

Hall, Jane and Dixie Haywood. *Precision Pieced Quilts Using the Foundation Method*. Radnor, PA: Chilton, 1992.

_____. *Perfect Pineapples*. Lafayette, CA: C & T, 1989.

Khin, Yvonne M. *The Collector's Dictionary of Quilt Names and Patterns*. New York, NY: Portland House, Publishers, a division of Dilithium Press, Ltd. Distributed by Crown Publishers, Inc., by arrangement with Acropolis Books Ltd. (reprint), 1988. Originally published by Acropolis Books, Washington, D.C., 1980.

Malone, Maggie. *Classic American Patchwork Quilt Patterns*. New York, NY: Drake Publishers, Inc., 1977.

McKim, Ruby Short. *One Hundred and One Patchwork Patterns*. New York, NY: Dover Publications, 1962.

Mills, Susan Winter. *Illustrated Index to Traditional American Quilt Patterns*. New York, NY: Arco Publishing Inc., 1980.

Lady's Circle Patchwork Quilts. New York, NY: GCR Publishing Inc.

Quiltmaker. Golden, CO: Leman Publications.

Resources

During the course of my tie exploration and experimentation I discovered the following products which proved extremely useful. Look for them in your local quilt or fabric shop. This list includes addresses for your convenience.

Pfaff Sewing Machines
(especially Creative 7550)
Paramus, NJ

Madeira Threads
600 East 9th St., 3rd Floor
Michigan City, IN 46360
Cotona #50, Bobbinfil #70, Variegated threads, Rayon #200

Mundial Inc.
Fifty Kerry Place
Norwood, MA 02062
#406-7 Dressmaker Shears, #202-5 Sewing Scissors, #427-4 Embroidery Curved, #301C Thread Clipper

Freudenberg Nonwovens,
PELLON Division
20 Industrial Avenue
Chelmsford, MA 01824
PELLON® #ES114 Easy-Shaper® fusible interfacing for light to midweight fabrics; PELLON® #93ITD fusible interfacing for mid to heavyweight fabrics; PELLON® Stitch-N-Tear®, rip-away backing for machinery embroidery & appliqué; *PELLON® Thermolam Plus®, heavily needled fleece

OMNIGRID, Inc.
1560 Port Drive
Burlington, WA 98233
The original black and yellow ruler

*Hobbs Bonded Fibers
Craft Products Division
PO Box 3000
Mexia, TX 76667
Hobbs Heirloom Cotton Batting, Hobbs Polydown Bonded, and Hobbs Thermore

Janet B. Elwin, Quilts Etc.
Prentiss Cove, HCR 64, Box 012
Damariscotta, Maine 04543
Hexagon and necktie patchwork skirts, 3 skirt variations – flared skirts with fitted or elastic waists, large pockets and pocket openings (no zippers), and uneven hem line. Dress or cotton fabric skirts have hexagon insets along the bottom edge. Necktie skirt can be lined or unlined.

Mail-order catalogs suggested by several guest quilters:

Keepsake Quilting
Route 25B, Post Office Box 1618
Centre Harbor, NH 03226-1618

Clotilde Inc.
2 Sew Smart Way B8031
Stevens Point, WI 54481-8031

*All the quilts made by the author for this book use Hobbs Heirloom Cotton Batting for large pieces and PELLON® Thermolam® Plus for small pieces. I recommend these as they machine quilt beautifully.

AQS Books on Quilts

This is only a partial listing of the books on quilts that are available from the American Quilter's Society. AQS books are known the world over for their timely topics, clear writing, beautiful color photographs, and accurate illustrations and patterns. Most of the following books are available from your local bookseller, quilt shop, or public library. If you are unable to locate certain titles in your area, you may order by mail from the AMERICAN QUILTER'S SOCIETY, P.O. Box 3290, Paducah, KY 42002-3290. Customers with Visa or MasterCard may phone in orders from 7:00–4:00 CST, Monday–Friday, Toll Free 1-800-626-5420. Add $2.00 for postage for the first book ordered and $0.40 for each additional book. Include item number, title, and price when ordering. Allow 14 to 21 days for delivery.

2282	**Adapting Architectural Details for Quilts,** Carol Wagner	$12.95
1907	**American Beauties: Rose & Tulip Quilts,** Marston & Cunningham	$14.95
4543	**American Quilt Blocks: 50 Patterns for 50 States,** Beth Summers	$18.95
2121	**Appliqué Designs: My Mother Taught Me to Sew,** Faye Anderson	$12.95
3790	**Appliqué Patterns from Native American Beadwork Designs,** Dr. Joyce Mori	$14.95
2122	**The Art of Hand Appliqué,** Laura Lee Fritz	$14.95
2099	**Ask Helen: More About Quilting Designs,** Helen Squire	$14.95
2207	**Award-Winning Quilts: 1985-1987**	$24.95
2354	**Award-Winning Quilts: 1988-1989**	$24.95
3425	**Award-Winning Quilts: 1990-1991**	$24.95
3791	**Award-Winning Quilts: 1992-1993**	$24.95
4593	**Blossoms by the Sea: Making Ribbon Flowers for Quilts,** Faye Labanaris	$24.95
4697	**Caryl Bryer Fallert: A Spectrum of Quilts, 1983-1995,** Caryl Bryer Fallert	$24.95
3926	**Celtic Style Floral Appliqué: Designs Using Interlaced Scrollwork,** Scarlett Rose	$14.95
2208	**Classic Basket Quilts,** Elizabeth Porter & Marianne Fons	$16.95
2355	**Creative Machine Art,** Sharee Dawn Roberts	$24.95
1820	**Dear Helen, Can You Tell Me?...All About Quilting Designs,** Helen Squire	$12.95
3870	**Double Wedding Ring Quilts: New Quilts from an Old Favorite**	$14.95
3399	**Dye Painting!** Ann Johnston	$19.95
2030	**Dyeing & Overdyeing of Cotton Fabrics,** Judy Mercer Tescher	$9.95
3468	**Encyclopedia of Pieced Quilt Patterns,** compiled by Barbara Brackman	$34.95
3846	**Fabric Postcards: Landmarks & Landscapes • Monuments & Meadows,** Judi Warren	$22.95
2356	**Flavor Quilts for Kids to Make: Complete Instructions for Teaching Children to Dye, Decorate & Sew Quilts,** Jennifer Amor	$12.95
2381	**From Basics to Binding: A Complete Guide to Making Quilts,** Karen Kay Buckley	$16.95
1982	**Fun & Fancy Machine Quiltmaking,** Lois Smith	$19.95
4526	**Gatherings: America's Quilt Heritage,** Kathlyn F. Sullivan	$34.95
2097	**Heirloom Miniatures,** Tina M. Gravatt	$9.95
2283	**Infinite Stars,** Gayle Bong	$12.95
2120	**The Ins and Outs: Perfecting the Quilting Stitch,** Patricia J. Morris	$9.95
1906	**Irish Chain Quilts: A Workbook of Irish Chains & Related Patterns,** Joyce B. Peaden	$14.95
3784	**Jacobean Appliqué: Book I, "Exotica,"** Patricia B. Campbell & Mimi Ayars, Ph.D	$18.95
4544	**Jacobean Appliqué: Book II, "Romantica,"** Patricia B. Campbell & Mimi Ayars, Ph.D	$18.95
3904	**The Judge's Task: How Award-Winning Quilts Are Selected,** Patricia J. Morris	$19.95
4523	**Log Cabin Quilts: New Quilts from an Old Favorite**	$14.95
4545	**Log Cabin with a Twist,** Barbara T. Kaempfer	$18.95
4598	**Love to Quilt: Men's Vests,** Alexandra Capadalis Dupré	$14.95
2206	**Marbling Fabrics for Quilts: A Guide for Learning & Teaching,** Kathy Fawcett & Carol Shoaf	$12.95
4514	**Mola Techniques for Today's Quilters,** Charlotte Patera	$18.95
3330	**More Projects and Patterns: A Second Collection of Favorite Quilts,** Judy Florence	$18.95
1981	**Nancy Crow: Quilts and Influences,** Nancy Crow	$29.95
3331	**Nancy Crow: Work in Transition,** Nancy Crow	$12.95
3332	**New Jersey Quilts – 1777 to 1950: Contributions to an American Tradition,** The Heritage Quilt Project of New Jersey	$29.95
3927	**New Patterns from Old Architecture,** Carol Wagner	$12.95
2153	**No Dragons on My Quilt,** Jean Ray Laury	$12.95
3469	**Old Favorites in Miniature,** Tina Gravatt	$15.95
4515	**Paint and Patches: Painting on Fabrics with Pigment,** Vicki L. Johnson	$18.95
3333	**A Patchwork of Pieces: An Anthology of Early Quilt Stories 1845-1940,** complied by Cuesta Ray Benberry and Carol Pinney Crabb	$14.95
4513	**Plaited Patchwork,** Shari Cole	$19.95
3928	**Precision Patchwork for Scrap Quilts,** Jeannette Tousley Muir	$12.95
3308	**Quilt Groups Today: Who They Are, Where They Meet, What They Do, and How to Contact Them – A Complete Guide for 1992-1993**	$14.95
4542	**A Quilted Christmas,** edited by Bonnie Browning	$18.95
2380	**Quilter's Registry,** Lynne Fritz	$9.95
3467	**Quilting Patterns from Native American Designs,** Dr. Joyce Mori	$12.95
3470	**Quilting with Style: Principles for Great Pattern Design,** Marston & Cunningham	$24.95
2284	**Quiltmaker's Guide: Basics & Beyond,** Carol Doak	$19.95
2257	**Quilts: The Permanent Collection – MAQS**	$9.95
3793	**Quilts: The Permanent Collection – MAQS, Volume II**	$9.95
3789	**Roots, Feathers & Blooms: 4-Block Quilts, Their History & Patterns, Book I,** Linda Carlson	$16.95
4512	**Sampler Quilt Blocks from Native American Designs,** Dr. Joyce Mori	$14.95
3796	**Seasons of the Heart & Home: Quilts for a Winter's Day,** Jan Patek	$18.95
3761	**Seasons of the Heart & Home: Quilts for Summer Days,** Jan Patek	$18.95
2357	**Sensational Scrap Quilts,** Darra Duffy Williamson	$24.95
3375	**Show Me Helen...How to Use Quilting Designs,** Helen Squire	$15.95
1790	**Somewhere in Between: Quilts and Quilters of Illinois,** Rita Barrow Barber	$14.95
3794	**Spike & Zola: Patterns Designed for Laughter...and Appliqué, Painting, or Stenciling,** Donna French Collins	$9.95
3929	**The Stori Book of Embellishing: Great Ideas for Quilts and Garments,** Mary Stori	$16.95
3903	**Straight Stitch Machine Appliqué: History, Patterns & Instructions for This Easy Technique,** Letty Martin	$16.95
3792	**Striplate Piecing: Piecing Circle Designs with Speed and Accuracy,** Debra Wagner	$24.95
3930	**Tessellations & Variations: Creating One-Patch and Two-Patch Quilts,** Barbara Ann Caron	$14.95
3788	**Three-Dimensional Appliqué and Embroidery Embellishment: Techniques for Today's Album Quilt,** Anita Shackelford	$24.95
3931	**Time-Span Quilts: New Quilts from Old Tops,** Becky Herdle	$16.95
2029	**A Treasury of Quilting Designs,** Linda Goodmon Emery	$14.95
3847	**Tricks with Chintz: Using Large Prints to Add New Magic to Traditional Quilt Blocks,** Nancy S. Breland	$14.95
2286	**Wonderful Wearables: A Celebration of Creative Clothing,** Virginia Avery	$24.95